"The only people mad at you for speaking the truth are those living a lie."

-Unknown

Other Books by Makaila Renee

THE TEARS I'VE CRIED: A Personal Memoir
GOOD TOUCH BAD TOUCH
THE LITTLE PRAYER BOOK
TALES FROM THE V.I.P ROOM

Coming Soon…

HEAR MY TESTIMONY (The Sequel to *The Tears I've Cried: A Personal Memoir*)

Special Preview of *Hear My Testimony*- page 153

Books published by Kaila's Playhouse

40 DAYS & 40 NIGHTS A SAINT

The Pursuit of Righteousness

Makaila Renee

An Original Kaila's Playhouse Edition
BALTIMORE, MARYLAND

An original **Kaila's Playhouse** Edition
Baltimore, Maryland 21201

This book is a work of non-fiction, based on true events.
Copyright © 2015 by Makaila Renee

ISBN-13: 978-0-9916204-6-3
ISBN-10: 0-9916204-6-1

First Kaila's Playhouse printing- June 2013

Manufactured in the United States of America

Cover design by Makaila Renee

DEDICATION

This book is dedicated to my God of Creation and His Holy Son.

— Makaila Renee

ACKNOWLEDGMENTS

I would like to acknowledge those who have supported my artistry and have been good to me regardless of my belief in God. Mama Susan Tappan-Black, Ms. Iris Blue, Natema Atlas, Dubonae and Maylica Haywood, Chondra Renae, Tobias Sanders, Moreno McCalpin, Glen Izett, Fabian, Timothy Mance, Shomari and Tim Johnson, Josh Johnson, Alicia Vasquez, Cousins Aquisha, Mario, Martez and Jennifer. Lawerence Carr also known as Christian St. Croix also known as Falton Carr also known as Harpo also known as whatever alias your using these days, thank you all for your inspiration and words of encouragement. I also wish to acknowledge the people who made me feel good and helped to keep me uplifted during my stronghold, such as Evangelist Anita Fuentes, Enoch Glover, Firecharger, FOTM1, Seth L, Warningthepeople, and all of my YouTube friends that I subscribe to. All of you have helped me keep a smile on my face in hard times (though you may not know it). I look forward to meeting with all of you, very soon.

—Makaila Renee

40 DAYS & 40 NIGHTS
A SAINT: The Pursuit of Righteousness

BASED ON TRUE EXPERIENCES

TABLE OF CONTENTS

A BRIEF INTRODUCTION

I am Makaila Renee, author, mother, fellow sinner and follower of Jesus Christ, the Son of God. When I say God, I speak of the first One True Living God of Creation. I feel the need to be clear about the One whom I testify about. I wish that I could tell you that I was perfect and have lived in a morally upstanding way all of my life, but that would be a lie. However, I can tell you that I have become an expert in endurance and in keeping the faith in God the Father and Christ the Son. On my walk with Jesus, I have experienced much (both good and bad) and I would like to share some of those experiences with you.

I decided to write 40 Days & 40 Nights A Saint: The Pursuit of Righteousness as I was undergoing my spiritual journey of following Jesus Christ. For forty days and nights, I made the choice to give up the temporal things of this world. I wanted to seek God first, and earnestly try to pursue a life of righteousness before Him. It was not an easy task, but it was necessary. During that time, I struggled with many issues and I chose forty of those topics which I felt were most important to discuss with you.

I hope that my book will uplift and encourage others to continue to do good to one another and strive for righteousness and the light forever; to get up and keep moving regardless of how many times we may stumble and fall; to search for God and seek out His Kingdom until death, to gain life. This book is an expression of love towards all of my neighbors both righteous and wicked alike, regardless of age, ethnicity, race, sexual orientation or socio-economic status. I love and only want the best for all of you, no matter how you may feel about me. My goal is not to persuade you to think how I think or to do as I do, but rather to share with you the truth.

Of Our Spiritual Strivings

In reading Dubois' Of Our Spiritual Strivings, I was captivated by his description of man's soul being torn asunder, no less divided between two opposite and opposing worlds. This same description can also be applied to our spiritual walk with Jesus Christ. Our mind and heart is good, but our flesh is sinful. So then, I myself in my mind am a slave to God's law, but in my sinful nature a slave to the law of sin (Romans 7:25). For the flesh desires what is contrary to the spirit, and the spirit what is contrary to the flesh. They are in conflict with each other (Galatians 5:17), thus I find my body and soul torn asunder, divided between two opposite and opposing strivings.

"He does not believe that does not live according to his beliefs."
-Sigmund Freud

Our most important, yet difficult challenge as followers of Jesus Christ is learning to master ourselves through self-control. We will never be able to fight off the enemy's seductive temptations until we can first control our selfish, passionate desires. We must spiritually strive to merge this double consciousness (soul and body) into one cohesive better and truer self. In order for this to happen, one of our dueling counterparts must be denied. Either we will allow the body (our flesh) and all of its lustful desires to rule over us, or we will allow the soul to rule, denying the flesh; thus the division of body and soul may finally be reconciled.

Sometimes we question how we are to follow the will of our Lord and savior in a corrupt world full of wickedness, without being seduced or tempted by worldly things? I have found that the only answer is to stay in the Word of God. We know who runs this world (Satan), but only for a short time (Revelations 12:12). The devil has but a limited time to drag as many souls off to hell before the master of the house who created it, will send his holy Son to reclaim it. Until that day, we will walk in the valley with joy, but also with caution. The system is set up to trap us in sin at every turn, therefore we must put God before us in every decision we make, asking the God of Creation to guide us and lead us from temptation. In any case, what it all boils down to is this: Will we choose to do His perfect will, or our own?

Why the God of Creation?

After some deep thought about how I came to meet God, I've come to realize that my finding Him was not an accident, but rather part of my destiny which had finally been fulfilled. The Lord, who had written my name in the Lamb's Book of Life, had known me since the day of creation, though I had not always known Him.

My discovering of our Lord and savior Jesus Christ was purely by accident (or so I thought) and took place while I was attending college in Tennessee. As a teenager, I had always loved stepping and had even organized a step team at Mira Loma High School in Sacramento, California where I grew up. So naturally, when I saw the steppers who were part of the Greek organizations at a local college, I wanted to partake in the festivities thereof. Eager, I went home that afternoon ready to research these organizations since I had never been the type to jump head first into anything without having the full scope of what I was getting myself involved in. From all that I had seen and heard about these Greek organizations, I felt that I would be best fitted to become a Delta, although a woman I looked up to as a mentor at the time was a member of the Alpha Kappa Alpha sorority. The more I delved into researching these Greek sororities, the more I became fascinated with the different gods and deities that each group worshiped and prayed to. Even though I was deeply intrigued, what struck me as odd what the fact that peoples of African descent were members of Greek organizations. Also, I knew some of these members to be Christians, and although I wasn't religious, even I knew that you cannot serve two gods as you would love one and hate the other (Luke 16:13).

After a while, I soon ceased in my research about sororities and began to focus my attention on researching different gods, deities and religions. Truthfully, all of this only gave me a headache. Deep down, I always knew that there was a God or something that created us, but I was unsure as to who's or what particular god reigned supreme.

There were two main inciting incidents that not only set my life changing decision in motion, but also exposed how all of my life experiences had led to this moment. The first incident involved an encounter with a Christian woman who was a former sorority member (about my age) that grew up in a very religious family. The woman told me her story of how she became critically ill after invoking a particular god (she called an idol) into her body. She noted that each time she would chant and pray to this idol, she was overcome with a feeling of sickness. Feeling in her gut that something wasn't right, she confided what she had been doing to her parents and her pastor. The woman's parents instantly became angry with her. They scolded her and berated her for bowing down in worship and prayer to a foreign god, then her parents whisked her off to their pastor for counseling and deliverance. The woman's pastor told her that by praying to this other deity, that she in essence was rejecting the Holy Spirit that all of us were born with, thus making room for this false god, which was no god at all, to govern her spiritually. The pastor went on to advise the woman to repent and renounce the organization that she was involved in, and pray to the God of Creation to restore and strengthen the Holy Spirit which had been convicting her. After doing so, the woman told me that she was finally well enough to return to school. I must admit that her story creeped me out a little, but I was glad she shared it with me in light of my desire to join such a group.

The second inciting incident involved my brief interaction with an atheist, believe it or not. I was on the subway in Baltimore when I heard this man ranting and raving to his friend about how stupid it was to believe in Jesus Christ, a God that no one alive in present times has seen and in his opinion, didn't exist. The man was talking so loud and aggressive, that it was evident to everyone that he badly wanted to be heard. So, I listened. The more this man spoke, the more I began to question why he was going so out of his way to bash and insult a man (Jesus) whom he said doesn't exist anyway; yet he was speaking of Christ as though He in fact did live. As I watched the atheist get angrier and angrier as he went on and on about someone who allegedly never was, it struck me as strange. Lots of people did not believe in the abominable snowman, the loch ness monster, big foot and UFO's, but I never hear any of them hatefully lecturing the people who have these beliefs like they do to followers of Christ Jesus. I was beginning to think that there could be some truth in this Jesus character.

Spring break was almost over and I was due to return to Tennessee to finish up my studies and prepare for my graduation that year. It was in BWI airport where I believe that I had my first supernatural encounter. While I was waiting for my flight to come in, a fair skinned black guy

came and sat down next to me. For nearly an hour, I spoke
with this stranger about everything under the sun from the
weather, to family, to work and God. I'm not sure how our
conversation transitioned to God, but I was astonished by the
wisdom this man had on the topic. It seemed to me that he had
special insight that made me feel genuinely interested about
the Lord. Granted, I attended church when I was a kid, but for
the first time in my life, I wanted to know more about God.
Sheepishly, I confided to the stranger that I didn't even own a
bible (I'm not sure why this embarrassed me), then I asked
him what chapters he liked best. The stranger threw his head
back and laughed like I would imagine Santa Claus would
have laughed if he were real. "For you, you'll start with the
book of Romans," he said. "Romans?" I repeated to him in
time for the airport lady to announce the arrival of our flight.
The stranger and I said our goodbyes and wished one another
well. Giving me one last glance over his shoulder with a smile
and a wave of the hand, he boarded the plane just minutes
before I did. I was impressed by this mysterious stranger and
inspired by our conversation. I wanted to thank him for his
company. When it was my turn to board the plane, I searched
every face from the first seats to the last in search of the man,
but he was nowhere to be found. I had actually planned on
sitting next to him. I loaded my carryon bag overhead, waited
for everyone to be seated and then walked the entire length of
the plane. I still did not see him. Later, when the plane landed
in Memphis, I was the first to grab my bag and exit. I stood in
the terminal and watched as every passenger got off the plane,
except the stranger that I was seeking. I had never believed in
ghosts, but suddenly I convinced myself that he had to have
been one. Eventually, I did get a bible, reading the book of
Romans first just as the stranger recommended. Later, I read a
passage in the book of Hebrews that said "Do not neglect
hospitality because through it some have entertained angels

without knowing it." So I chalked up my experience with the mysterious stranger at BWI as an encounter with an angel or messenger sent by God.

The more I read my bible, the more I began to like and developed respect for the God of Creation. What really made me choose Him was the fact that He was first. I imagined how disrespected He must feel to have created man, only for them to turn around and spit in His eye, creating false gods to worship from materials that He made. In my mind, I sort of compared it to a mother who gave birth to a child, only to later be rejected by the child who would later call another woman 'mother'. The more I considered these things, the more agitated I became with the ungratefulness of mankind. Never the less, I was eager to begin communication with God because I felt I was still missing something and I needed to know for sure if this God thing was real. According to His holy Word, I needed to go through His One and only Son Jesus Christ to get to Him (the Father). Like most people, I prayed to God in the past when I found myself in trouble, but from then on, I prayed to Him earnestly and without doubt.

Who's Who: The Father, The Son & The Holy Spirit

God

God is the creator of the heavens, the earth and all that is in it including you and I. This Creator God that I speak of is the One True Living God. To know God, you must first have an understanding of the supernatural for He is spirit and His spirit is Holy. Our Heavenly Father knows our deepest inner thoughts and He knows our hearts. Though we sometimes try to mask ourselves to one another, we cannot fool God. Many people see God as a punisher, but in reality He is so loving that he sent His Only Son as a living sacrifice to atone for our sins. In this way, we who choose Him will live and not die, though we were born sinners.

The Son

Jesus Christ is the Son of God and our only hope for salvation lies in Him. The Son of God has the keys of life and death and it is He alone who shall judge men (and women) of the earth. Jesus is God in the flesh, meaning that our Heavenly Father has poured out His Holy Spirit into His Son. The Son of God intercedes for us when Satan stands before the Father with reason to drag our soul off to hell. Similar to a defense attorney, Christ is there to step in on our behalf and remind our Father that there is still hope for us yet. Patient, the Son of God hopes that we will confess our sins and repent. It is only through the Son of God that our sins and trespasses are forgiven and wiped out forevermore. The mission of the Son of God is to set the captives (us) free by the teaching and practicing of the Word of God. It is my belief that God may have poured out His Holy Spirit into Christ Jesus, a man, so that through the Son, He may know the temptations and trials of men. In any case, without the Son of God, those of us seeking the thrill of immortality could never attain it.

The Holy Spirit

The Holy Spirit is a spirit that is indeed Holy. The Holy Spirit is no joke and is NOT to be played with, taken lightly and certainly not denied. To be filled with the Holy Spirit is a feeling like no other. It's not so much as a physical feeling, but a knowing or realization that your life has forever changed. To be baptized with the Holy Ghost means that you have been spiritually renewed and are born again. Though you may not have done away with your old ways, under the new influence of the Holy Spirit, who convicts us and guides us, you will eventually do what is right.

Crucifying the Flesh

It has been my experience that without crucifying the flesh, meaning to deny the flesh of its sinful lusts and passions, you will not see the Father of Creation pour out His full promise upon you. We must live in the Spirit, not the flesh, allowing the will of our Heavenly Father's to prevail over our own. Because God is of the Spirit and we are born of the flesh, we have the free will to make a choice. We can decide to live by the Spirit, or continue to live by the flesh. Our mind and soul craves an intimate relationship with Jesus Christ, yet our bodies crave worldly things (sex, drugs, alcohol, gambling and any other thing we put before our Lord and Savior, which in essence is a form of idolatry). I myself recognize that I have been living in the flesh as of late. For I know that in my flesh dwelleth no good thing.

"He who controls others may be powerful, but he who has mastered himself is mightier still."
-Lao Tzu

"If you conquer yourself, then you conquer the world."
-Paulo Coelho

For I have the desire to do what is right, but not the ability to carry it out (Romans 7:18). I know that I have to sacrifice marijuana and curb my sexual desires lest I'll be overcome by my flesh. Starting tomorrow, I will begin the task of murdering my flesh, making no provisions for it (Romans 13:14) at all. I do not expect that this will be an easy task, but one that I must take on none the less. Don't get me wrong, our Heavenly Father still blesses us while we are sinners, but imagine how much more he will bless those who seek to do His will!

"Know thy enemy and know thy self and you can fight a hundred battles without disaster."
-Sun Tzu

The Chastening

Last night, my soul was tormented something terrible! Never in my life had I experienced being tortured supernaturally. All night long I suffered the fiery darts, slings and arrows. Satan and his agents wore me out and would not allow my soul rest, yet that is their job and I cannot blame them for doing the work that is theirs. I awoke with various mysterious scratches, knicks and cuts on my body. The experience was a real spiritual wakeup call as I realized that I was being chastened, or disciplined.

Chastening can occur in many different forms such as physical illnesses, broken relationships, loss of peace, and other unpleasant or negative circumstances. For whom the Lord loves he chastens (Hebrews 12:6). We should not despise the Lord's discipline or resent His rebuke,

"In the midst of affliction He counsels, strengthens confirms, nourishes and favors us... Moreover, when we have repented, he instantly remits the sins as well as the punishments."
-Martin Luther

because the Lord disciplines those He loves as a father the son he delights in (Proverbs 3:11-12). The will of our Heavenly Father is for all of us to live holy lives. When we who are born again choose to dwell in sin and do not resist temptation, He chastens us in order to redirect our path to Him. Instead of blaming God for my torment, I blame myself for giving the devil a foothold in my life to begin with. Although I had given up marijuana, the devil found other sin dwelling within me: that of sex and my tongue, which I have not guarded. It was my inequities that opened for him a door to harass me. Experience has shown me that God will use chastening as a way to send us a sign that we are not operating according to his will, so that we may come to repent and obey Him.

Disturbed yet awakened, I resolved to cast away these demonic spirits and entities I wrestled with for Christ's sake. Because I understand that some unclean spirits do not come out except through fasting and prayer (Matthew 17:21), that is precisely what I will do. I will fast and pray all day long. I will repent, confess my sins to the Lord and meditate on His Word all day. I believe in the Word of God and have faith in His truth. I am certain that fasting and prayer, combined with

"The Lord gets His best soldiers out of the highlands of affliction."
-Charles H. Spurgeon

confession and repentance will give me relief from these unclean spirits that assail me day and night. Also, going forward, I will try to carefully guard my speech. Taming the tongue is one of our most difficult tasks as humans, but especially for someone like me. I grew up in a poor crime-riddled environment filled with blunt communicators who used profanity freely. Even so, just as I overcame my addiction and vengeful ways, I have full confidence that I too can overcome my wild tongue victoriously through Christ, who strengthens me. I am fully aware that the only reason that I suffer this mental, physical and spiritual torment is because of my disobedience to our Lord, yet there is still hope. Our Heavenly Father knows my heart. Due to my unshakeable faith in Him combined with my own will being set against my inequities, He will sustain us even through strongholds. Praise and glory to the Lord our God forever and ever. Amen

Sinners Rescued

ATTENTION SINNERS: Every day that the God of Creation wakes you up, there remains the hope of salvation in Jesus Christ for you. Remember the story of our ancestor Abraham. In the fifth chapter of the book of Romans, we find that Abraham received the seal of righteousness from God while he was still uncircumcised (unrighteous). So how did Abraham, an unrighteous man receive the seal of our Lord and savior? He received grace from God not by his works, but by his faith in the Lord, which was accounted to him as righteousness (Romans 4:9). The reason the God of Creation blessed Abraham in this way was so that he might be the father of all those who believe, thought they too are uncircumcised (unrighteous), and that righteousness might be imputed to

"I am not a saint, unless you think of a saint as a sinner who keeps on trying."
-Nelson Mandela

"So when the devil throws sin in your face and declares that you deserve death and hell, tell him this: "I admit that I deserve death and hell, what of it? For I know One who suffered and made satisfaction on my behalf. His name is Jesus Christ, Son of God, and where He is, I shall be also."
-Martin Luther

them also (Romans 4:11). Therefore, although we sin, if we have faith in the Lord and believe, we too can receive the promise of God granted by faith. Some of you have no clue about the power that one righteous person holds, but I do, and that is why I strive for righteousness every day and with every breath that I take. Did you know that our Heavenly Father will even deliver one who is not innocent by the purity (cleanliness) of your hands (Job 22:30); or that based on the testimony of two or three witnesses, a person can be redeemed or put to death (Deuteronomy 17:6 & 2 Corinthians 13:1); or that the prayers of a righteous man avails much (James 5:16); or that one righteous person can destroy the works of ten thousand demons; or that the unbelieving husband is sanctified by the wife, and the unbelieving wife is sanctified by the husband (1 Corinthians 7:14); likewise, once the God of Creation establishes His covenant with you, He will also establish the same with your children. Once this covenant is established, even if your children goes astray or abandons the faith, God will chasten him (or her) with the rod of men, but not destroy them. For these reasons, I strive for righteousness and hold onto my faith in Jesus Christ. I wish to be counted among the saints who shall return with our Lord and Savior on judgement day. I will continue to keep my hands clean and do no harm to my neighbor. In this way, my family and friends who are not so innocent may be delivered through the purity of my hands. I also wish to be one of the two witnesses testifying on behalf of them so they too will be redeemed. I pray that the God of Creation will also sanctify my husband and children, establishing His covenant with them on my behalf. All of these things I want not only for my benefit, but for yours as well because I love you. Though I do not know some of you, I care for you so much that I would lay for you- if the cause is right and just.

The reason Jesus Christ has compassion on those who are ignorant and have gone astray is because He Himself is also subject to weakness (Hebrews 5:2). My fellow sinners, please erase the fears you have about Jesus sitting on high waiting to pounce on you and throw you into hell because of your sins. Jesus came into the world to save sinners, not to destroy them. The account of the apostle Paul who used to persecute, jail and murder followers of Christ further illustrates God's forgiveness and mercy towards sinners. Never forget that by one man's disobedience (Adam and Eve), many were made sinners, so also by one man's obedience (us) many will be made righteous (Romans 5:19), but a sinner can only be saved by grace, not by works alone. Have faith in the Father God, the Son and the Holy Spirit. Amen

And What of Gay Folk

How dare you take away the Son of the One True Living God from gay folk? How dare you? Who do you think you sinners are? Was Christ not sent to die on the cross for us all? Did our Lord and Savior value one man's soul over another's? How dare you judge someone else's servant? To their own master, servants stand or fall (Romans 14:4), and many of us can barely even master ourselves.

Nothing grieves me more than to hear one sinner condemning another because of their sin. Frankly, it sickens me to the core. He who saith that they are not a sinner is a liar and the truth is not in him (1 John 1:8-10). At the end of the day, no sin is greater or lesser than the other, meaning that one who tells a lie, one who steals, one who commits adultery and one who fornicates stands on no morally higher ground than he or she who engages in homosexual activity. Any and every sinner regardless of which sin they commit is in danger of going to hell if they do not confess their sin and repent; as it is written that the wages of sin is death (Romans 6:23). Many gay folks have lost hope and faith in the Lord Jesus Christ because they have been brainwashed by people who constantly condemn them to hell for their sin. We have absolutely no right or authority to do this. Tis faith in Christ that carries one not so innocent into the Kingdom of Heaven. Satan does a well enough job of lying and deceiving and convicting us without our help. Unless you are the devil's agent, please stop condemning our neighbors, but love them (not their sin) instead. Let's face it, gay folk are not stupid at all. They know that they are sinning same as you and I know that we too sin. Do not crush their hopes of salvation as you and I also hope to be saved by our faith. Truth be told, this entire time that I have suffered and been persecuted for my faith in Jesus Christ, not one from the gay community has stretched out their hand to harm, oppress or condemn me. It has been around true lovers of Christ and gay folk that I have felt most safe. Perhaps this is because they too have been ridiculed, harassed and beat down by society, that they dare not do the same to their neighbor.

Am I standing up for homosexuality? No, I'm standing up for humanity who have all been born sinners and all have fallen short of the glory of God (Romans 3:23). When Jesus Christ commanded us to love our neighbor, He did not say love our straight neighbor, or love our neighbor that does not lie or steal. The words 'love thy neighbor' means precisely what it says. That said, love thy neighbor, but not thy neighbor's sin. Judgment belongs to Him who died on the cross and shed His blood to atone for the sinners of the world. Again, we have no authority whatsoever to judge anyone at all. Quit trying to do God's job by judging your neighbor regardless of what sin they commit. Of course it is good to warn your neighbor once or twice, afterwards, leave them alone. God did not need our help to create the heavens and the earth and all that is in it, and He certainly doesn't need our help in judging any one of His children. We don't even have the power to wake up on our own, let alone the authority of condemnation over our brothers and sisters. If we are truly concerned for our sinning neighbor, we must pray for them, then leave the matter in God's hands. It is most crucial that we concern ourselves with minding our own affairs and getting our own houses in order for the sake of Christ's return. Also, I am well aware that many may condemn me as well for practicing God's law of love for all of my neighbors (not their sins), but I careth not. Only God can judge me- not you, my dear fellow sinner. Amen

We Are One

Allow me to answer that age old question by saying, "Yes, you are you're your brother's keeper," and we are all responsible for one another because we are one. Race, ethnicity, age, gender, sexual orientation and socio-economic status matters not to the God of Creation who created us equal, valuing no person's soul over another's. Nobody on this earth is better or more superior than their neighbor. Sure someone may be youthful, have more education, or money- big deal! Their sense of superiority over you is all in their delusional mind. Likewise, your sense of inferiority to them is all in your mind. According to our Heavenly Father, what makes

"An army of the people is invincible."
-Mao Tse-tung

"Be of one mind and one faith that you may conquer your enemies and lead long and happy lives." - Genghis Khan

"I cut myself in the finger and it pains me: this finger is a part of me. I see a friend hurt and it hurts me, too: my friend and I are one. And now I see an enemy stricken down, a lump of matter which, of all lumps of matter in the Universe, I care less for, and it still grieves me. Does this not prove that each of us is only part of a whole? For ages this idea has been proclaimed in the consummately wise teachings of religion, probably not

us one nation under God is our faith and belief in Jesus Christ. There is no Jew nor Greek, slave nor free, male nor female, for you are all one in Jesus Christ (Galatians 5:2628). Just as the body has members (arms, legs, feet, etc.,), so does humanity. Some of us are strong, some weak, some secure, some insecure, some good, some wicked. In any case, we are parts of a whole as creations of God. Should the foot say, "Because I am not the hand, I am not of the body (1 Corinthians 12:15)?" Should the righteous man say to the wicked, "You are not a creation of God?" The Word of God tells us that there are many members, yet one body (1 Corinthians 15:20), and we are one. Know this: Although we are individuals, if one member suffers, all the members suffer with it; if one member is honored, all the members rejoice with it, therefore we all are our brother and sister's keeper with a responsibility and an obligation, towards one another's salvation or lack thereof. If you see that your brother or sister is falling and you do not help to lift them up, then you partake in their demise. If you see your neighbor sinning and do not at least warn them, their blood will be on your hands. The most important thing that connects us is that we were all born sinners. And while we were still sinners, Christ Jesus died for all of us (Romans 5:8), not for a select few.

"We must become bigger than we have been: more courageous, greater in spirit, larger in outlook. We must become members of a new race, overcoming petty prejudice, owing our ultimate allegiance not to our nations but to our fellow men within the human community."
-Haile Selassie

alone as a means of insuring peace and harmony among men, but as a deeply founded truth. The Buddhist expresses it in one way, the Christian in another, but both say the same: We are one."
-Nikola Tesla

What Is Success?

According to the Merriam-Webster
dictionary, success is described as
getting or achieving wealth, respect or
fame. Most people, especially in
America view success as being rich or
famous, but what is success to you,
and how far are willing to go to attain
it? In my opinion, success is a matter
of perspective. I perceive success as
having peace, happiness and stability
of mind and living circumstance. In
my spiritual journey with Christ Jesus,
I have learned to be satisfied with the
simple things in life. As long as my
children and I have food or clothing, I
consider all else that may come to me
as a blessing from the Lord Almighty.
This does not mean that I do not aspire
to reach higher, for I know what I am
capable of and I fully expect to soar to
greater heights as I seek ye first the

"He who
wishes to be
rich in a day
will be hanged
in a year."
-Leonardo da
Vinci

"It is not titles
that honor
men, but men
that honor
titles."
-Niccolo
Machiavelli

Kingdom of God. Never the less, if I cannot be happy and have satisfaction with what is little, then I will never be satisfied with much. Consider how many wealthy people are never truly satisfied with all that they have, so that they continuously chase after more and more. They buy for themselves a mansion, but envy their neighbor who has a castle. The wealthy woman see's the huge diamond ring on her neighbor's hand and goes home to nag her husband for a bigger one yet. Rarely will the monetarily rich be satisfied with all of their riches gained by their own hands without God. The sleep of the laboring man is sweet, whether he eats little or much; but the abundance of the rich will not permit him to sleep Ecclesiastes 5:12). All his days he also eats in darkness, and he has much sorrow and sickness and anger (Ecclesiastes 5:17) because of his ungratefulness and longing for more abundance. What good does it do a man to labor in vain all his life when he cannot take any of his worldly possessions to the grave? We all are born naked, and naked we shall leave this earth. The best of riches come from the hand of our Heavenly Father. Only the Lord knows what some people have done to get to where they are. Many have strayed far from the faith and have no problem robbing and oppressing the poor, or stepping on their neighbor's neck on their way to

"Of mankind we may say in general that they are fickle, hypocritical and greedy of gain."
-Niccolo Machiavelli

"If you want to succeed you should strike out on new paths, rather than travel the worn paths of accepted success."
-John D. Rockefeller

"How many Emperors and princes have lived and died and no record of them remains, and they only sought to gain dominions and riches in order that their fame might be everlasting."
-Leonardo da Vinci

what they deem to be the top. Money may not be the root of all evil, but the love of money certainly is (1 Timothy 6:10). And just how much do you love money? Would you be willing to sell your soul to the devil himself, for it? And what do you benefit if you gain the whole world and lose your own soul (Mark 8:36)? Better a poor and wise youth, than an old foolish king who will be admonished no more (Ecclesiastes 4:13).

In no way, shape or form am I implying that our Lord wants us to be poor- to the contrary! When we delight in the Lord Jesus Christ and commit our work to Him, He gives us all the desires of our hearts (money, peace, happiness, good health, etc.) and our plans will be established (Psalm 37:4 & Proverbs 16:3). No place in the bible or in the Words the Lord has ever spoken to me does He express His desire for us to live poor. Therefore, humble yourselves to the Lord and He will exalt you. One who is faithful in a very little is also faithful in much, and one who is dishonest in a very little is also dishonest in much. If you have not been faithful in unrighteous wealth, who will trust you with true riches (Luke 16:10-11)?

At the end of the day, we have approximately seventy some odd

years to live on this earth (less than that if you are poor or
unhealthy), but eternity is forever. Should we really spend the
short time that we have chasing ill-gotten riches, or in
disobedience to the God who created us and will give us
riches and eternal life in Paradise? Throughout the second
chapter of Ecclesiastes, the son of David describes how he
had obtained all that his eyes and heart desired. He was not
only a great man in the eyes of our Heavenly Father, but he
also excelled more than all who were before him in
Jerusalem. Yet Solomon hated all of his labor which he had
toiled under the sun, for he must leave it to the man who will
come after him. The success of this world is fading and
temporary, but the rewards from the Lord are everlasting. It is
the Lord our God that gives us power to get wealth, that He
may confirm his covenant that He swore to your fathers, as it
is this day (Deuteronomy 8:18). Allow the Lord to make you
abundantly prosperous as He took delight in prospering your
fathers before you. Therefore, I tell you do not be anxious
about your life, what you will eat or drink, nor about the
clothes that you put on. Is life not more than food and the
body more than clothing? Look at the birds of the air that
neither sow nor reap, and yet you're Heavenly Father feeds
them. Are you not more valuable than they (Matthew 6:25-
26)? Trust in the Lord that he will fulfil His promise of great
success for you, for unlike man, He cannot tell a lie. Follow
Christ and wait patiently knowing that everything has its time
and season to come to pass. Even if it seems slow, wait for it
without doubt in your heart about receiving it; for it will
surely come; it will not delay (Luke 2:3). Amen

Take Courage

The main reason many of us become stuck in the same cycles is because we often lack the courage to change. We are so worried about what mom and dad will think or concerned about what our friends would think if we were to step outside of the 'norm'. As great as it is to be considerate of others feelings, their impressions and opinions of us should not outweigh that of God, who has created us. As much as we love mommy and daddy, they do not have the ability to save our soul, but only the Son of God can. Also, in as much as we rely on the assistance of our family, friends, spouses and loved ones, can we not rely on God's help even more so? I only ask this so that you may determine who is really pulling the strings that control our lives. What type of hold on you do these people

"The darkest places in hell are reserved for those who maintain their neutrality in times of moral crises."
-Dante Alighieri

"Cowards die many times before their actual deaths; the valiant never taste of death but once."
-Julius Caesar

have on you to influence you so deeply? Surely we owe mom and dad our loyalty and respect for bringing us into this world, but our lives belong to the God of Creation who sent us unto them. No person or thing should have more control over our lives than our Lord and Savior.

There are several reasons why we want to change, but do not. The most common reason that people refuse to change is fear of rejection. We fear that if we suggest that a change be implemented at work, that our idea may not be well received by our boss. We worry that if we switch our college major to a more fulfilling career path, we may disappoint our parents. If we change our hair, clothes or image in any way, or deviate outside of what is considered to be normal, we may lose our friends. Change (even positive change) may leave you feeling ostracized from a sheep-like society. You might even be viewed as a rebel and could be rejected by all but those with leadership mentalities. It is astonishing that we want to fit in *so* badly with the peoples of this corrupt world, that we are willing to risk our salvation in Jesus Christ without even knowing it. Many people want to change, but lack the courage to do so. To this I say take courage friends. Do not be afraid of

"I learned that courage was not the absence of fear, but the triumph over it. The brave man is not he who does not feel afraid, but he who conquers that fear."
-Nelson Mandela

"The loss of liberty is less than the price of repression."
-W.E.B Du Bois

"Never was anything great achieved without danger."
-Niccolo Machiavelli

"Not only will we have to repent for the sins of bad people; but we also will have to repent for the appalling silence of good people."
-Martin Luther King Jr.,

change and reformation of the spirit/soul.

Another thing it takes courage to do is to stand up for God. Far too many people have become easily manipulated and deceived by ungodly propaganda. Promoting dark secrets, these people have knowledge of the wickedness in this world, but rather than distancing themselves from what will lead them to the grave, they have become willing participants in dark agendas that lead to destruction. Instead, we must take courage, turning away from evil and humble ourselves unto the Lord. The Lord our God said: "Have I not commanded you? Be strong and of good courage; be not afraid; neither be dismayed: For the Lord thy God is with you wherever you go" (Joshua 1:7). Therefore, pray for the courage to take a stance against evil, simply by not participating in dark agendas.

Please listen to me friends for I tell you the truth. Not my truth, but *thee* truth, and I realize that the truth can be a hard pill to swallow. Sometimes the truth can hurt our feelings, embarrass us, expose us or enlighten us, yet it is the truth none the less and cannot be denied. Everything I tell you, I say out of love and concern because you are my neighbor. At the end of the day- no, at the end of your life, do you want to go to heaven or do you want to go to hell for an eternity? If you want to go to hell, fine. Toss this book over your shoulder and keep it moving or give it to someone with more common sense than you have. If you want to enter the Kingdom of God (regardless how mow much or little faith you have that you will enter into it), the first thing we need to do is confess and repent. Then we can walk in this world not with our tail tucked between our legs, but as the fearless beings that our Father has created us to be. When you see evil hatching before your eyes, do not bury you head in the sand, but walk away from it. Whether you speak out against wrong or turn away from it, the Lord see's that you are taking a stance against it. Let's face it, you are either for the God of Creation, or against Him, and if you are still straddling the fence, you are not for God.

Yet, there is still hope until the day your immortal soul leaves its shell (the body). Every day that the God of Creation wakes us up brings forth new chances, new choices to make and new tests to pass. Set your goal on doing better today than you did yesterday (even if it's just slightly better). The internet is full of testimonies from former Satanists and occult members who have changed their ways and given their lives back to Christ Jesus. "We can also bear in mind the testimony of the apostle Paul, formerly known as Saul of Tarsus who persccuted, opprcsscd and murdcred hundrcds of God's people before becoming one of God's elect:

"For you have heard of my former conduct in Judaism, how I persecuted the church of God beyond measure and tried to destroy it. And I advanced in Judaism beyond many of my contemporaries in my own nation, being more exceedingly zealous for the traditions of my fathers. But when it pleased God, who separated me from my mother womb and called me through His grace, to reveal His Son in me, that I might preach Him among the Gentiles… (Galatians 1:1316)."

Again, it takes courage and a strong will to change and anyone who lacks these things should seek them from Christ. I tell you straight up, that this is a matter of life and death. If you do not care about your own life, how then about the lives of your family? Will you selfishly drag the souls of your sons and daughters off to hell with your own? The time is now that we must take a stand and fight for our eternal lives. I tell you my friends, do not fear those who can kill the body and after that do no more (Luke 12:9). Rather fear Him which is able to destroy both body and soul in hell (Matthew 10:28). Amen

The Falling Away

One **evening**, I lie in bed contemplating the falling away from God. I could not fathom why the very people that God created would grow distant from Him, some even to the point of hating or denying Him. No matter how hard I tried, it was difficult for me to make sense out of what I deemed to be senselessness, but still, I was seeking understanding. In order to wrap my boggled mind around this, I decided to conduct in depth research on the issue, as well as draw from my own experiences from the valley. Though my research does not apply to every person's individual case, here is what I found to be most common:

Although every human born on this earth is unique, I find that there are three major groups as it pertains to the belief or nonbelief in the existence of God:

1. The Atheist, who does not believe in what he or she cannot physically see or touch. In their hearts, they strongly believe that there is no God of creation, let alone acknowledge that He has a Son. Ironically, they *do* believe in the existence of places and countries that they have never physically seen or stepped foot on based on books they have read or testimonies given to

them by others. Still, ironically they refuse the testimony given in books and people about the God of Creation or the Son of God.

2. The Apathetic, are those that neither doubt, nor confirm the existence of God the Creator in their hearts. I was a former member of this group.

3. The Believer, who knows by faith, personal relations or otherwise that the God of Creation is real and true. Whether the believer is for or against God, they still acknowledge His existence.

Though the first two groups are against God, all of these groups have in common the hope of salvation promised to them through Jesus Christ (because you are either for God or against Him). When we examine the falling away or turning from the God of Creation, we can identify four major groups:

A. I'll call 'Born into it', meaning that their beliefs have been passed on from one generation to the next.

B. The 'Dabblers', meaning they have been exposed gradually to things that are not of God the Creator (Satanism, occults, spiritualism, etc.). Some dabblers have testified that they feel they have somehow gotten in to deep and feel somewhat trapped into the lifestyle or fearful of the repercussions of turning away from such a lifestyle.

C. Groups C & D are both 'Embracers', yet these groups differ from one another. Group C are the embracers by choice, meaning that they have made a conscious decision to choose darkness over the light, hating both God the Creator and His followers. Many of these embracers, like Saul of Tarsus, have been chosen by God to do His work, though they do not know it, yet.

D. Group D represents the second type of embracer, who has also made a conscious decision to go against God, but, this embracer will never know or pursue a relationship with their creator. This type of embracer refuses to turn from evil because they are content with a life in the dark. This embracer will spend their eternity in hell for their intentional and willful stubbornness and wickedness.

The beauty of it all is that groups A, B & C all have hope for salvation in the Lord Jesus Christ, but it takes courage and a strong will to change. I propose that the only way we will ever get out of the hellish pit we have dug for ourselves is through the confession and repentance of our sins to obtain forgiveness and be freed from our pasts. If we confess our sins, He is faithful and just to forgive us our sins and to cleanse us from all unrighteousness (John 1:9). This means that the Lord must, and will forgive anyone who comes to Him, no matter what they have done. The more evil and wicked you have been, the happier the God of Creation will be that you have returned to Him, for it is in His Word and He is not a liar (Numbers 23:19).

Beware of Wolves

During my walk with Jesus Christ, nothing has gotten under my skin more than wolves in sheep's clothing. Even more than the loss of family, friends, material possessions, and more than my distain for lying familiar spirits and nosy people, wolves in sheep's clothing have bothered me most because of the level of deception involved. They are the traitors of whom Dante Alighieri and the God of Creation warns us about that will receive the greatest of punishments in the blackest depths of hell, which is reserved for them and fallen angels. There is none more despicable than a person who smiles in your face, wearing a mask of friendship and sincerity to hide their treacherous and malicious true nature. Posing as a friend or helper, they trick unsuspecting people. And no wonder! For Satan himself transformed himself

"Everyone sees who you appear to be, few really know what you are." -Niccolo Machiavelli

"There is nothing more important than appearing to be religious." - Niccolo Machiavelli

into an angel of light (2 Corinthians 11:14).

The Word of God tells us that we do not wrestle against flesh and blood, but against principalities, against powers, against rulers of the darkness of this age, against spiritual hosts of wickedness in the Heavenly places (Ephesians 6:12). Who is it that rules the darkness of this age and who are the spiritual hosts of wickedness? Satan rules the darkness of this age and people, who are in reality children of God, have been taken captive by the devil to do his ungodly will. The prince of darkness has blinded these people who are used as his puppet slaves, which is why they do not listen to or believe the gospel of Christ. He who is of God, hears God's words; therefore, they do not hear because they are not of God (John 8:47). They are of their father the devil (who has ensnared them) and the desires of their father, they want to do (John 8:44). Beware of these seducers, tempters, deceivers and wolves in sheep's clothing, but inwardly they are ravenous wolves. These imposters will grow worse and worse, deceiving and being deceived by Satan. (2 Timothy 3:13).

Despite the fact that these wolves disguise themselves in sheep's skin, you will still know who they are by their fruit (actions). For they are lovers

"A tyrant must put on the appearances of common devotion to religion. Subjects are less apprehensive of illegal treatment of a ruler whom they consider God-fearing and pious. On the other hand, they do less move against him, believing that he has the gods on his side." - Aristotle

"A vulgar crowd is always taken by appearances, and the world consists chiefly of the vulgar." -Niccolo Machiavelli

"You gotta be careful of the company you keep."
-Dave Chappelle

of themselves, lovers of money, boasters, proud, blasphemers, unthankful, unloving, unforgiving, brutal, slanderers, traitors, without self-control, despisers of good and lovers of pleasure rather than lovers of God. They have a form of godliness as they are made in His image, yet God is not in their hearts (2Timothy 3:2-5).

In an ideal world, everyone would be open about who they are, what they are about and what they believe. Though I do not condone gayness, I can at least respect someone who is open about their sexuality, instead of hiding who they are. In the same way, I cannot respect a closet homosexual who marries a woman purely for a front to disguise his true nature or sexuality. But I digress. I suppose I can be somewhat of an idealist at times, but only in a perfect world would wolves truly reveal themselves to us. I guess if we knew who these wolves were and what they were truly about, that would take the fun out of deceiving us, as Satan has deceived them. The only reason people of darkness hate people of the light is because our light exposes their wickedness. For everyone practicing evil hates the light and does not come to the light, lest their evil deeds should be exposed (John 3:20). From such people turn away!

Finally, in avoiding such divisive persons, I urge you to note who is causing drama and division and avoid them. For those are such that do not serve our Lord Jesus Christ, but their own belly, and by smooth words and flattering speech deceive the hearts of the simple. For your obedience to God had become known to all. Therefore, I am glad on your behalf, but I want you to be wise to what is good and simple concerning what is evil. And the God of peace will crush Satan under your feet shortly. The grace of Jesus Christ be with you. Amen

Tithes

One **of the biggest scams** in the church today is the tithing deception. The tithing deception in essence, is stealing from the poor. Unfortunately, when people are lost, sick, hurting and looking for hope, it is easy for greedy church leaders to deceive its members into thinking that they must give them their money or worldly possessions in exchange for the cure of salvation which they themselves cannot provide. It is not my intention to discourage church members to stop giving to their church, in fact I think that's wonderful. I do encourage church leaders to stop preaching on tithes which do not belong to the church, and request contributions and donations for the church instead. Friends, your tithes should not go to the church, but to your poor and needy

"Do you know that God entrusted you with that money (all above what buys necessities for you and your families) to feed the hungry, to clothe the naked, to help the stranger, the widow, the fatherless; and indeed, as far as it will go, to relieve the wants of all mankind?"
-John Wesley

"I have attended church since I was a week old. I've listened to sermons about virtue, sermons about vice. I have heard about money, time management, tithing, abstinence, and generosity. I've listened to thousands of sermons. But I could count on one hand the number of sermons that were a simple proclamation of the gospel of Christ."
-Rich Mullins

neighbors. It is the elderly person, the widow, the fatherless child or any other poor and needy member of your community to whom your tithes should go. There is a beautiful illustration in the bible where Jesus speaks to His chosen ones who will inherit the Kingdom of God: "For I was hungry and you gave me meat; I was thirsty and you gave me drink; I was a stranger and you took me in; I was naked and you clothed me; I was sick and you visited me; I was in prison and you came unto me (Matthew 25:35-36). Then the righteous answered the Lord, saying, "Lord, when did we see you hungry and feed you? Or thirsty and give you drink? When did we see you a stranger and take you in? Or naked and clothed you? Or when did we see you sick and in prison and came to visit you?" And the King shall answer and say to them, "Verily I say unto you, in as much as you have done to the least of my brethren, you have done it to me (Matthew 25:37-40)." In other words, when we help lift up our poor or needy neighbors, we lift up our Lord Jesus Christ. No place in the bible or in the words the Lord has given unto me does He say to give your tithes to your spiritual leader. Some of these greedy men and women who deem themselves spiritual leaders will misquote and misinterpret the Word of God to deceive you and further their own agendas for selfish gain. Rather than simply asking church members to donate or contribute to the church, they misuse the word tithe to fool you. Many of these church leaders live in great mansions and castles, have several luxury cars, personal jets and other worldly possessions while their church members are struggling to pay their bills. Church members, let me ask you this: If you cannot pay your rent or mortgage, can you go to your church leader for help? If you have no food and your utilities are getting ready to be shut off, can you go to your church for assistance? If the answer to these questions is no, then perhaps it's time to reconsider who you are giving your tithes to, and what they are being used for. I have heard countless people say, "Well, I pay my tithes to the church, and whatever the church leader uses them for is between him (or her) and God." But I tell you today, that what *is* between you and God is your responsibility to your neighbors who need your help. Will you tell God, "I did not help my neighbors in need because I gave my church leader who is not in need, my money?" Our Lord and Savior Christ Jesus did not have a central location where everyone came to pay Him to preach the Word of God. Instead our Lord and savior came to us, going door to door, place to place and country to country, teaching and spreading the gospel free of charge. People did *contribute from their hearts* unto our Lord by way of money, food, a place for Him to rest, washing of His feet, etc. However, The Lord Jesus Christ did not request that the peoples give him ten percent of their earnings. There are few churches and church leaders that actually go door to door soul winning for Christ. When was the last time that your church or church leader went door to door soul winning? Some of the most popular bible verses that church leader use to manipulate church members comes from Malachi 3:8-10.

This verse explains that the Lord is angry and feels He is being robbed because people are not bringing tithes and offerings to the storehouse so that there will be food in His house. Many church leaders will argue that the church is the storehouse, but it is not. The storehouse that our Lord and savior spoke of was not a church, but an actual storehouse that benefited poor people and the saints. Please remember that the Lord's entire ministry was based on healing the sick and giving to the poor. Allow me be to be frank with you: If your church or church leader is not healing you or giving unto you when you are in need, then their ministry is pointless, fruitless, dead and without substance- point blank, period. I'll go further to say that the reason many church leaders are not healing you, is because they do not have healing abilities. Many of them have appointed themselves as church leaders without God's approval or anointing. This could be the reason that you walk into church sick and depressed and you return home in the same condition. Also bear in mind that some church leaders may not be physical healers, but they are spiritual healers, and that is great. We all need to uplift one another spiritually and continuously.

Another popular bible verse used to scam you of your hard earned money comes from 2 Corinthians 9:6-9 which states, "Remember this: whoever sows sparingly, will also reap sparingly, and whoever sows generously, will also reap generously. Each man should decide in his heart what to give (Not what he is pressured to give by church leaders), not reluctantly or under compulsion, for God loves a cheerful giver. And God is able to bless you abundantly, so that in all things at all times, having all that you need, you will abound in every good work. As it is written: They have freely scattered their gifts to the poor; their righteousness endures forever." Folks, unlike many of your spiritual leaders, our Lord and savior is not just speaking in terms of money when

He tells us that we will reap what we sow. When we are kind to each other, we reap what we sow, receiving kindness in turn. When we do our neighbors dirty, and someone in turn wrongs us, we have reaped what we have sown. If you have extra food or clothes and give them to the homeless or poor, our God in heaven will see it and indeed you will reap what you have sown. What many church leaders do is convince you into believing that if you tithe unto them your money, that God will return it to you. If your church leader is poor or needy, then you are doing him a great service and God will bless you for it because tithes are supposed to go to the poor and needy. On the other hand, if your church leader is wealthy, why are you giving him your tithes when there are poor and needy people sitting right beside you in the church? They are literally waiting on the Lord and His people to bless them. Not to mention all of the needy folk in your community that you drove pass on the way to your church.

Last month, I watched a video on YouTube that completely disgusted me. The video showcased two popular pastors running around the church, literally dancing on piles of money that their members were throwing at their feet. One of the two pastors preached a full sermon on tithing alone, stating (and I quote),

> "…Somebody said, I didn't come here because I want to hear about money, I came here because I want some peace. Well honey, you need some money or you ain't never gonna know no peace." The pastor went on to say (and again, I quote), "I heard people say: It's not about money, it's about peace and it's about joy and it's about love," slapping the bible he carried he says, "No! It's about money!"

I could not believe my ears, and to that I say "The devil is a liar!" I showed the same video to my fourteen year old daughter, then asked her what she thought about what she had seen. I did not tell her what I thought about the clip because I

did not want to give her any preconceived notions. I wanted
her open and honest child-like perspective. My daughter
shook her head and said, "Geez, they sure love money." Then
she added, "I'm surprised they have so many church
members, talking like that." People, if a fourteen year old
child can discern this scam, why are so many adults taken in
by it? Maybe spiritual maturity does not come with age, but is
gifted through the Holy Spirit.

Now, I do not mean to pick on church leaders, I'm
simply calling it as I see it and telling you the truth. I keep in
mind that many of these leaders do not really know any
better, for they grew up tithing to the church the same way
that we have. They are simply using the same traditional
practices that they grew up in, and that's fine. But there are
also many leaders that know better. They have knowledge
that tithing is to the poor and do not care. It is they who
disgust me and anger our Lord and Savior Jesus Christ with
their blatant manipulation of what is good for their own gain.
Rather than encouraging church members to give freely from
the heart as Christ did, they demand ten percent of their
church member's monies. Although many of them would
make great motivational speakers, they are not preachers of
the One True Gospel of Christ. Anyone can give a lecture
about human conduct and prosperity, but what of confession,
repentance and the love of Jesus Christ?

Many people think of tithes in terms of money, but that is
only a small part of it. Tithes can be our clothing, crops, and
any other fruits of our labor produced from the land, weather
grain from the soil or fruit from the trees (Leviticus 27:30).
These things are holy to the Lord. Now, if you still choose to
think of tithing in terms of money only, that's your
prerogative. Just be sure you tithe unto the Lord, not your
church leader as they are not your God... or are they? As
previously stated in Matthew 25:35-40, we clearly see how
we can serve our Lord and Savior in His absence by tithing

to our poor and needy neighbors. Do not ever forget that Satan also tried to use bible verses to tempt, manipulate and deceive Jesus Christ in the wilderness (Matthew 4:3-6). The gospel of Christ is to be told, not sold.

Idol Worship

How long will some of you
continue to worship the creation and
not the Creator? Have you ever
considered how the God of creation
feels to watch you bow down to His
creations in worship? Some of the
things that I am about to tell you, you
will not like because I know that many
of you have been worshiping idols for
a long time and may not be receptive
to correction. My desire is not to make
anyone feel foolish, but in being
truthful with you, I will not hold back
the truth due to the severity of the
topic. I will not hide how much it
sickens me that the children of God
have the audacity to make for
themselves idols of carved images to
call their God. According to the
Merriam-Webster dictionary, an idol
is nothing more than an image or other

"Do not
worship me, I
am not God. I
am only a man.
I worship
Christ."
-Haile Selassie

"You were destined to worship God and if you fail to worship Him, you will create other things (idols) to give your life to. You are free to choose what you surrender to, but you are not free from the consequence of that choice."
-Rick Warren

"Men are so simple and so much inclined to obey immediate needs that a deceiver will never lack victims for his deceptions."
-Niccolo Machiavelli

man-made material object representing a deity *other* than God; a false God. It is a person or thing regarded with blind admiration, adoration or devotion; a mere semblance of something visible, but without substance, as a phantom; a figment of the mind; fantasy; a false conception or notion; a fallacy. Yet, this is what the children of the One True Living God have chosen to worship… a false god. All of this seems silly to me, a chasing after the wind.

Why would you take a beautiful tree that God has created, and carve from it an idol or a false god? The wood has no eyes to see, no ears to hear, no legs to walk and no life within. A block of wood, marble, granite, silver, gold, clay or whatever the God of Creation has made has no ability to save you, yet you make from it images of bulls, calves and two headed monstrosities with multiple arms and legs to call your god. The Word of God warns us of such practices throughout the scriptures. I remember taking a wood shop class in high school. I made an astray and a coffee mug, but never did I consider carving an image to call it my God. Even at a young age, I was smart enough to recognize that a statue of any kind could never be anything more than what it was. Sadly, I'm willing to bet that if I carved an image of a man and a woman from wood, that I could convince some of you that these images were your parents. I figure that if you will believe these mad-made images to be god, then I can convince you to except them as anything I like. Let me tell you plainly: God made man, man cannot make God. Therefore, your man-made images and sculptures are not gods at all. You shall not make idols for yourselves; neither carved images or a sacred pillar, alter or engraved stone to bow down to it; for I am the Lord your God (Leviticus 26:1). The God of Creation will not give His glory to, nor share it with carved images (Isaiah 42:8). Furthermore, the One True Living God of Creation tells us to give no regards to mediums and familiar spirits; do not seek after them to be defiled by them: I am the Lord your God (Leviticus 19:31). Our Heavenly Father goes on to say that the persons who turns to mediums and familiar spirits, to prostitute himself with them, He will set His face against, and cut that person off from his people (Leviticus 20:6). Should not a people (created by the Creator, not the creation) seek their God? Should they

"What could be more hapless than a man controlled by his own creations? It is surely easier for a man to cease to be a man by worshiping man-made goods than for idols to become divine by being adored."
-Augustine of Hippo

seek the dead on behalf of the living (Isaiah 8:19)? Now the
Spirit expressly says that in latter times, some will depart
from the faith, giving heed to deceiving spirits and doctrines
of demons (1 Timothy 4:1), but each time you do so, you
provoke God into anger and dig your own grave deeper and
deeper.

But there is still hope for the idol worshiper, as there is
hope for any other sinner who is blessed to live another day.
The thirty-third chapter of the second book of Chronicles tells
us the story of King Manasseh's redemption after idol
worship. At twelve years old, Manasseh became king of
Jerusalem and did evil in the sight of the Lord. He rebuilt and
raised up the alters for Baal that his father Hezekiah had
broken down. He made wooden images to worship, practiced
soothsaying, used witchcraft and sorcery and even caused his
sons to pass through fire in the valley of the Son of Hinnom.
Manasseh even had the nerve to set up one of his carved
images in the house of the Lord, seducing Judah and the
inhabitants of Jerusalem to worship false gods and do evil.
Now the Lord our God spoke with Manasseh and his people,
but they would not listen. Therefore, the Lord brought upon
them the army of the King of Assyria who took Manasseh
captive with hooks, carrying him off to Babylon. In great pain
and affliction, Manasseh humbled himself and prayed to the
One True Living God of Creation who heard his request and
brought him back to Jerusalem and into his Kingdom. Then
Manasseh knew that the Lord was God. Doing a complete
one-eighty, Manasseh destroyed the pillars and alters of Baal,
the carved images, took away the foreign gods from the house
of the Lord and cast them out of the city. Manasseh continued
to pray and make sacrifices of peace to the God of Creation
until his death. His prayers of how God received him, wiping
away his trespasses after the evil he had done were written
among the sayings of Hozai. In contrast, Amon, Manasseh's

twenty-two year old son who became king did all the evil that his father had done, but Amon did not humble himself before the Lord as his father did. As a result, his servants conspired against him and killed him in his own house.

We need to think long and hard about our choices before it is too late. Many of you who worship idols are my true friends and I know you to be good people. You have treated me better than some of my blood relatives even though you know that I stand with Christ. That said, I would be disloyal to you, God and myself in pretending that idol worship is not wrong. It really pains me to see people destroy their lives and the lives of their families behind idol worship. Keep in mind that the artists who made these images are just as imperfect as you and I. They are sinners like you and I and if I were you, I would not entrust my fate in their hands nor the creations that they make. I definitely will not twist anyone's arm into seeing things my way. I simply decided to address the issue because I care about you.

Sex

I **write this letter** to discuss sexual immorality, one of the biggest and most difficult demons that I have ever had to conquer. I'm sure that our great great-great-great-great grandparents can tell us of a time when sex was a sacred act between a man and his wife, but now, all we need to do is turn on the television, radio or take a short walk around the corner to see how sensationalized that sex has become. Sex, and suggestions of sex are everywhere around us. I went to the store to buy a water bottle for my daughter to take to school. Instantly, my eyes are drawn to a hot-pink (my favorite color) bottle with a round top and ridges up the sides. The water bottle was shaped like a man's penis, and I certainly was not going to allow my daughter to put her mouth on it. I went into another store to buy my daughter her first purse so she would

"I count him braver who overcomes his desires than him who conquers his enemies; for the hardest victory is over itself."
-Aristotle

finally leave mine alone. There was this one particular purse was shaped like a lingerie top and even had two breast-shaped lumps. I discovered the purse in the junior's section, and was almost afraid to find what may be lying in wait in the women's section.

Now, let's turn on the television. I do not need to tell you about all of the sexual subliminal messages and sexual suggestions in television commercials, programming and in films. Sure I like bananas- I think they're delicious, but eating one is not an orgasmic experience as it was for the woman I saw eating one on television. Since when do we need to lick a banana up the side of it and moan before taking a bite off the top? Many of us have seen the 'kissable lipstick' advertisement in the movie, *Boomerang*... Need I say more? How many sex scenes and other scenes of intimacy between unmarried couples do you and your children watch on a daily basis?

Sexual suggestions are powerful seeds that both the youth and adults water with their hopes, dreams, passions, desires and fantasies. With the increase of sexually explicit images on television and in films, we can no longer blame the twelve year old girl who has had more sexual partners than we adults have had. So, what does our Heavenly Father say about sex? For this is the will of God, your sanctification: that you should abstain from sexual immorality (1Thessalonians 4:3). The main reason God views fornication and adultery as such an ugly sin is because every sin that man does is outside the body, but he who commits sexual immorality sins against his own body (1 Corinthians 6:18) which is the temple where the Holy Spirit lives. Therefore, not only do we sin against our own body, but we also sin against the Holy Spirit within us. Our bodies are to be presented as clean sacrifices to Christ, pure of sex, smoke and anything else which harms the body.

The only way to avoid sexual temptation is to flee it.

No longer can we afford to put ourselves in a position that would compromise our will to abstain. When I listen to sexually suggestive music, I get really horny, then I start to fantasize about sex, so I had to start guarding my ears. On the other hand, I can watch sexual scenes on television and they have no effect on me at all. Some people listen to music with violent undertones and begin to feel angry or amped up, but others are not affected. The only reason I'm disclosing these things to you is to make you aware of different emotional triggers that can lead us astray and down the wrong path. I think we all should be aware of what stimulates and motivates our actions. A smoker gets stressed and grabs for a cigarette; an addict sees a needle on the pavement and is tempted to get high. Know your sexual triggers.

I also wanted to discuss marriage with you. If you have been with your mate two years or more, perhaps it is time to get married or move on. I have seen far too many common law marriages in the United States. Many of these couples have been together seven, thirteen, twenty years, but are still unmarried. Before I truly knew God, I myself was in a seven year relationship with my children's father without marriage. The reason the God of Creation instructs young women and widows to marry is because He understands our strong sexual needs (1 Timothy 5:11-14) and would rather have us unify in marriage than to engage in random sexual relations. I encourage anyone who has been in a long term relationship to do what is right and get married right away. If you do not have a lot of money, go down to your local courthouse, jump a broom or simply take your marital vows under the stars before God. Do whatever is in your heart to please God and wipe away your sin, now. You can always have the wedding of your dreams later, Lord willing that you live to see another day.

We all know it's wrong to fornicate and commit adultery,

so there's no need to drill each other about it, but let me say a few more things on the matter. In my walk with Jesus Christ, no harsher chastening and punishment ever came upon me as when I was fornicating. When I was having premarital sex, I experienced more pain, more sickness, more persecution and more hardships, than when I had been abstaining. I believe it is because deep down, I knew better and the Holy Spirit inside me was convicting me. I was doing my own selfish will, not the Lord's, and His mighty hand came down on me like a ton of bricks. This is how it shall be in the last days: Seven women shall take hold of one man, saying, "We will eat our own food and wear our own apparel; only let us be called by your name, to take away our reproach (Isaiah 4:1)."

Spirits Are Real

Spirits are very real and go under a variety of names, like ghosts, demons, apparitions, poltergeist, shadow people, etc. No matter how you look at spirits, one must recognize that they are either godly or ungodly spirits. Godly spirits include the Spirit of wisdom and understanding, the Spirit of counsel and might, and the Spirit of knowledge and fear of the Lord (Isaiah 11:2). Are they not all Spirits sent forth to minister to these who will inherit salvation (Hebrews 1:14)? There is no grey area when it comes to good and evil spirits.

Not only are spirits real, but they also have the ability to transfer from one host (person, animal and thing) to another. Throughout the bible, there are several illustrations of Jesus Christ casting out demons or unclean spirits with a word, in addition to healing

"No I never saw an angel, but it is irrelevant whether I saw one or not. I feel their presence around me."
-Paulo Coelho

those who were sick (Matthew 8:16). This fact, only solidifies the existence of spirits and their capabilities to enter into and possess a person.

The fifth chapter in the book of Mark gives us a compelling testimony of the transferring of unclean, demonic spirits: Jesus comes to a demon-possessed man who dwelled in the mountains and in tombs, crying out and cutting himself. When he saw Jesus from afar, he ran and worshiped Him (as even demons submit themselves to our Lord and savior). And he cried out in a loud voice and said "What have I to do with you, Jesus, Son of the Most High God? I implore you by God that You do not torment me." Then Jesus asked him, "What is your name?" and he answered saying, "My name is Legion; for we are many." Also, he earnestly begged Jesus not to send him out of the country. Now a large group of swine was there feeding by the mountains, so the demon begged Him saying, "Send us to the swine that we may enter them." Once Jesus gave them permission to enter the pigs, and they did so, the heard of demon-possessed pigs ran down the steep mountains and drown in the sea. We can learn from this story about a demons quest to kill and destroy their hosts.

Still skeptical about the existence of spirits? Chat with a psychic or

"The day science begins to study the non-physical phenomena, it will make more progress in one decade than in all the previous centuries of its existence."
-Nikola Tesla

"Everything is possible, from angels to demons to economists to politicians."
-Paulo Coelho

"Our body is dependent on Heaven and Heaven on the Spirit."
-Leonardo da Vinci

someone who channels spirits of the dead and ask them who they are communicating with, and from where their information comes. Many popular actors and musicians (in television interviews) have spoken of invoking or channeling spirits into their bodies to enhance their performances, similar to the way an athlete might use steroids. Do as you please, but I have to admit that the idea of any spirit other than the Holy Spirit dwelling inside me, creeps me out. Also, once you give these unclean spirits permission to enter you, or open a door for them to come, they may continue to do so whenever they please, with or without your permission. Once inside, these demonic spirits can actually control, if not fully possess aspects of your personality and your actions. This I have witnessed with my own eyes. Have you ever seen a person being taken over by a spirit before your very eyes (not on TV, but in real life)? Trust me when I tell you that it is the most unnatural sight that one can behold. Know that the God of Creation is against such things and views the act of spirit channeling or invoking as an abomination to our temples (bodies). If God was not against such things, He would not have sent His Holy Son Jesus Christ to cast out such abominable spirits from His children. The Word of God says that if you receive a different spirit or gospel which He had not given you, that you may well put up with it (2 Corinthians 11:4). This does not mean that those practicing such activities are bad or evil, but they do need to stop what they are doing none the less if they want to live lives pleasing to their Creator God. Therefore, he who rejects this does not reject man, but God, who has also given us His Holy Spirit (1 Thessalonians 4:8). What kind of spirit(s) takes precedence in your life?

After I had been called to be used as a vessel for Christ Jesus, I found myself in the home of one that I had known to practice spirit invocation. After engaging in a wonderful conversation, the two of us started to watch a little television.

Everything was cool until my friend suddenly turned to me
and told me that the reason I was having trouble seeking
employment in my field (I have a degree in Communications
with an emphasis in television and film) was because 'I knew
too much' (too much about what, she did not say). She went
on to say that 'it would be best to keep my big mouth shut,
and stop looking on the internet at things that weren't meant
for me to see, and searching for things that weren't meant to
be found,' lest 'they' were going to kill me. I watched this
woman turn from friendly to hateful in mere seconds. I knew
her well enough to discern that she was being used as a host
for a spirit that I saw as being both fearful of me and
threatened by me for whatever reason. To be honest, I had no
clue why this spirit was accusing me. All of this was very
bizarre to me because I had no idea of what this spirit had
thought that I had seen, heard, knew or searched for, other
than a relationship with Christ. I thought to say something,
but the Holy Spirit within me urged me not to engage (or
feed) the unclean spirit within her. After a minute or so, my
friend continued to watch television as if nothing happened.
As I sat there thinking about what all of this meant, my friend
turns to me with a sad look on her face and asked me if I was
alright. Realizing that she was back to her senses, I told her
that I was fine, then asked her the same. I could see in her
face that something was bothering her. She laughed an
awkward laugh and said, "What were we just talking about
anyway?" I could tell that she was embarrassed. "Work," I
offered. It was obvious that she had no recollection of the
things she just spewed at me and truthfully, we had spoken of
employment prior to her outburst. Besides, I did not want to
hurt her. I did manage to make an excuse to leave early after a
bit more small talk though. At the time, I had no authority to
command that spirit to come out of her, and I certainly did not

wish to see what the spirit was capable of doing to me through her, if it were to return.

Unfortunately, that was not the first, nor the last time that an unclean spirit used someone around me to try to intimidate or harass me. I had had plenty of experiences with those who entertained familiar spirits (that often lie). In the past, I listened to family repeat portions of private conversations (word for word) that I had with my children. Co-workers would be given knowledge about things that had taken place in my house via these mischievous spirits. The danger of entertaining such spirits lies in the fact that these spirits are unholy, and not of the God of Creation, but of Satan. The apostle Paul testified that often times these spirits tell lies: "A thorn in the flesh was given to me, a messenger of Satan to buffet me, lest I be exalted beyond measure. Concerning this thing I pleaded with the Lord three times that it might depart from me. And He said to me, "My grace is sufficient for you, for My strength is made perfect in weakness (2 Corinthians 12:7-9).

Still convinced that these spirit guides, ancestral spirits and familiar spirits have your best interest at heart? Ignore then, turn away from them and stop following their advice, and I'll bet that all hell will break loose as these so-called good spirits quickly turn on you. Hundreds if not thousands of mediums have testified about this. For the life of me, I guess I will never understand why anyone would seek guidance from masquerading demons instead of the Holy Spirit gifted to us by our Creator, but to each his own. In any case, if you ever want to know the *truth* about me, it would serve you best to ask my (our) God.

Spiritual Warfare 101

Spiritual **warfare is the most** crucial issue in our walk with Christ, yet surprisingly, it is the least discussed topic in churches today. Spiritual warfare is defined as taking a stand (offensive or defensive) against evil forces (Merriam-Webster dictionary), but I wish to expand upon this definition by adding that spiritual warfare also deals with demonic bondages and the resistance, defeating and overcoming of the enemy's deceptions (lies), accusations and temptation. One of Satan's greatest tricks has been to make people think that he does not exist. If people do not believe in the existence of the devil, they cannot recognize when he is at work in their lives, let alone fight him off. If we believe that good exists in this world, how can we not believe that evil exists also?

In spiritual warfare, how and when

"Hence it comes about that all armed Prophets have been victorious, and all unarmed Prophets have been destroyed."
-Niccolo Machiavelli

"We make war that we may live in peace."
-Aristotle

"Before all else, be armed."
-Niccolo Machiavelli

"If ignorant of both your enemy and yourself, you are sure to be in peril."
-Sun Tzu

to engage is as important as when not to engage. Satan is fully equipped with tools of war and he has been using these tools to ensnare the souls of men in bondage since the beginning. Demonic bondage, deceptions, accusations and temptation are the main tools utilized by the devil, your adversary. It is important to not only know the tools of the devil, but how we can resist, defeat and overcome his snares in two ways: offensive and defensive warfare

Satan's Main Tools of War:
-Deceptions
-Accusations
-Temptation
-Demonic Bondages

1. **Deceptions (lies)** - Satan's native language is called lies and deceit and whenever he speaks there is no truth in him because he is the father of lies (John 8:44). One of the devil's most popular deceptions has been to convince people that they themselves are miniature gods of some sort, and therefore, do not need the One True Living God in their lives. This deception/illusion has been so strong, that although people recognize that they did not create themselves or their parents; that when they get sick, they seek a doctor as they cannot heal themselves; nor do they have the power to extend their lives another hour, still they fashion themselves as gods in their own eyes.

2. **Accusations**- The accuser (Satan) loves nothing more than to rub a sinners face in their past sin, making them

feel ashamed, beyond redemption and beating our spirit man down with guilt. Also, with accusations come condemnation (which I will get into in a moment, so bear with me). Since the begging of the world, we see that Satan has always been the accuser of man. In the day that the sons of man presented themselves before the Lord Almighty, Satan too came among them to accuse them of malice (Job 1:6). One of the devils most prevalent accusation whispered in the ears of all of us by Satan is, "Look at your past sins! Jesus Christ will never forgive you. Do you think that you can sell your soul to me, then turn away and return to your Heavenly Father who created you for himself? You've gone too far to turn back, now… blah, blah, blah." Well, we either can listen to the father of lies or trust the truth of Christ Jesus who died to wash away the sins of the world and everyone in it. The story Christ Himself tells us about the Prodigal Son and the testimony of the apostle Paul who used to persecute, jail and murder followers of Christ before his redemption shows us that Satan's accusations have no merit and are built on the foundation of lies (the devil's native language) to deceive us.

3. **Temptation**- Temptation is the devil's most frequently used tool used to ensnare our souls and lead us further from the perfect will of the God of Creation. It is also why we are all born sinners (due to Eve being tempted to eat of the tree of life). Satan knows all of our strengths and our weaknesses, and should he not? He has studied us all, well enough. Whatever your weakness, Satan will use it against you and tempt you based on it. Let's say that you are a man (or woman) with marital problems. You are simply not getting enough sex at home and it frustrates you with a passion. You see a gorgeous woman (or handsome man) drop a wallet as they rush to catch the subway. Now the enemy know that money is not your weakness (you have been working at the

bank for years), but sex is. You chase down the man or woman to return their belongings and they begin to flirt with you, showing legitimate interest and filling the empty void that your spouse has left unfulfilled. Next thing you know, the two of you are shacked up in some raunchy motel going at it like two jackrabbits. Sure this example may be a little far-fetched (maybe not), but you get my drift. At the end of the day, just know that the devil would never waste time using your strengths to tempt you. Since Satan uses our weaknesses to tempt us, we need to be aware of what our weaknesses are.

4. **Demonic Bondage**- Did you know that aspects of your personality and even some of your actions can be under the influence of demons? Anything that we have become a slave to (addiction, sex, work, gambling, etc.) puts us in bondage, and bondage is not of the God of Creation, but comes from Satan the oppressor. There was a time in my life when I needed a joint to start my day similarly to the way some folks need coffee. When I was stressed out, I needed a joint, when I wanted to celebrate, I needed a joint and when I wanted to sleep through the night, I needed a joint. I tried to stop smoking weed numerous times, but could never figure out why I kept going back to it. Although, I had dedicated my life to Christ Jesus, little did I know that there were still aspects of my life (flesh) that was under the influence of demonic oppression, which had me in bondage. Once I realized that I could not fight my addiction to marijuana by myself, I took my burden to a higher power (Jesus Christ) to seek help. Eventually, He did deliver me from that addiction, but it was in His own perfect timing, and not my own. Often times, we do not have the ability or power to resist, defeat and overcome demonic strongholds, but greater is He (God) that is in us, than he (Satan) who rules the world (John 4:4).

Two ways to deal with spiritual warfare:
Offensive- The Sword (The Word of God)
Defensive- The Armor (Application of the Word)

Offensive warfare tears down the enemy's strongholds, demonic bondages, deceptions and accusations that the devil has formed in our minds.

Defensive warfare guards and protects us against the enemy's tactics, schemes and strategies, making his tools useless.

Dealing with Deception: Stay in the Word of God. Offensively, the Truth (Word of God) is our most powerful weapon against Satan. Even Jesus Christ Himself used the Word of God to defeat the devil's attacks when He was tempted in the wilderness (Matthew 4:4-11). Each time Satan came at our Lord and Savior with a deception, Jesus used the words "It is written," followed by the Word of our Heavenly Father. If Jesus Himself uses the Word of God to defeat Satan, we should also do the same.

Dealing with Accusations and Condemnation:
Condemnation is a statement or expression of a very strong criticism (Merriam-Webster dictionary). Accusations and condemnation comes from Satan the accuser. On the other hand, Jesus did not come to condemn the world, but to save it (John 12:47). There is no condemnation in Jesus Christ (Romans 8:1). Therefore, when we hear someone say, "I know I'm going to hell," what that person is doing is exercising self-condemnation, which stems from the devil's deceptions and accusations. Now, if that same person says, "I want to go to hell," they are stating their desires and exercising their free will to make stupid decisions, not condemning themselves. The will of our Heavenly Father is that we are not to dwell on our pasts, which has passed away

(2 Corinthians 5:7), and our sins have been forgotten (Hebrews 10:17). Remind yourselves of this daily and meditate on it, so that you can tell this to the enemy the next time he comes to accuse you.

Dealing with Temptation: Submit yourselves therefore to God. Resist the devil and he will flee from you (James 4:7). Self-control and resistance is the only way to defeat and overcome the enemy's temptation. Know your weaknesses.

Dealing with Demonic Bondage and Strongholds: Faith in Jesus Christ will always put out the fiery darts of the enemy (Ephesians 6:16). Pray continuously to cast away the influences of demonic, unclean spirits. What have you been thinking? Perhaps it is time to take out the trash of negative thinking. We must be mindful of your thoughts as Satan loves to implant thoughts in your head so that you think they are your own thoughts. In spiritual warfare, there are two voices speaking two thoughts. Satan tells you that you are the worst of sinners, while Jesus Christ tells you that if you turn to Him that you will be forgiven (1 John 1:9). Whichever lie or truth you believe will constantly grow and be fed to you by the one who gives it to you. Thus the thoughts you think will affect how you feel, and how you feel will have an effect on your actions. God wants us to put away our former conduct, the old man which grows corrupt from deceit and lusts, and put on the new man which was created according to God, in true righteousness and holiness (Ephesians 4:22 & 24). We must become transformed by the renewing of our minds (Romans 12:2) to tear down demonic strongholds and become free of Satan's bondage. When we begin to acknowledge God in all of our ways, He will direct our paths (Proverbs 3:6).

The battle may be the Lord's (which He has already won), but we are still His soldiers! How to not to engage in spiritual warfare is as important as how to do so. When we rebuke

Satan, we do not do it in our own power, saying, "I rebuke you!" Instead, we are to rely on God's power, not our own, saying, "The Lord rebuke you!" The nineteenth chapter of the book of Acts amuses me greatly because it gives us the ultimate example of how not to engage in spiritual warfare:

"Some Jews who went around driving out evil spirits tried to invoke the name of the Lord Jesus over those who were demon-possessed. They would say, "In the name of the Jesus whom Paul preaches, I command you to come out." [14] Seven sons of Sceva, a Jewish chief priest, were doing this. [15] One day the evil spirit answered them, "Jesus I know, and Paul I know about, but who are you?" [16] Then the man who had the evil spirit jumped on them and overpowered them all. He gave them such a beating that they ran out of the house naked and bleeding (Acts 19:13-16).

The reason the seven sons of Sceva received such a beating was because they either did not know or truly believe in the Christ Jesus they spoke of, making their words empty, powerless and void of authority. Casting out demons or unclean spirits is at the highest level of spiritual warfare. Before you go to war with Satan and his demons, be sure to confess your sins and repent, knowing without a doubt that Christ has forgiven you, so that you will have the full authority over the demonic realm.

RECAP:

1. Rely on the power of the God of Creation, not your own.
2. Offensively, wage war with the sword (the Word of God).
3. Defensively speaking, protect yourself with the full armor of God (application of the Word).
4. Rebuke in the name of Jesus Christ, not your own.
5. Always keep watch for the tools of the enemy (deceptions, accusations, temptation, demonic

bondages), and pray continuously.

Other Tools Satan Uses:
- Media (music and television with subliminal messages and demonic agendas).
- People (Satan uses people to do his will, discourage, intimidate and harass)
- Games (Ouija boards, séances, horoscopes and tarot cards can be a portal that opens the door to the demonic realm: See Ouija board games gone wrong on YouTube)
- Religion (arguments about organized religion only divide God's people)
- Alcohol, Drugs and Pills (Satan uses addictions to keep you in demonic bondage, unaware and stagnated)

"The general who wins the battle makes many calculations in his temple before the battle is fought. The general who loses makes few calculations beforehand."
-Sun Tzu

Stop Kicking Dead Horses

This letter is addressed to the believers in Jesus Christ, the one and only Son of God.

I noticed that non-believers of Jesus Christ spend so much time to try and convince believers that God does not exist. At first, I could not understand why someone would put so much effort in disclaiming the existence of the Holy one. Then I realized it is because they are merely the natural man or natural woman, meaning that they can only comprehend what their eyes can physically see and their hands can physically touch. You the believer, are the spiritual man or woman who sees beyond what is temporal, but what is eternal. But the natural man or woman does not receive the things of the Spirit of God, for they are foolish to him; nor can they know them, because they are spiritually discerned (1 Corinthians 2:14).

"People talk to people who perceive nothing, who have open eyes and see nothing; they shall talk to them and receive no answer; they shall adore those who have ears and hear nothing; they shall burn lamps for those who do not see."
-Leonardo da Vinci

"The educated differ from the uneducated as much as the living from the dead."
-Aristotle

"Where there is shouting, there is no knowledge."
-Leonardo da Vinci

As a believer, I was always ready to convince any nonbeliever that Jesus Christ is real. I wanted to lead them to the truth so that they too may receive the free gift of eternal life (especially if that person was a loved one or someone close to me). I would spend hours debating with the spiritually void only to waste my time, breath and energy. In doing so, I was indeed casting my pearls before swine, which the bible explicitly tells believers not to do (Matthew 7:6). It took a while, but finally I realized that I, who had the Spirit of the One True Living God was arguing with the natural man who did not have the Spirit of God and therefore would not and could not comprehend spiritual matters no matter what I told them or how long I spoke to them. Only the God of Creation, His Son and the Holy Spirit can convince such a person of the truth. The natural man or woman cannot soar beyond the natural realm and has no spiritual discernment, so we believers need to stop kicking dead horses. It is right to warn our neighbors about the dangers of not having Christ Jesus (it our duty), but do not get caught up in playing a game of spiritual ping-pong with one who has not the Spirit of God. Remember: the fool says in his heart :There is no

God" (Psalm 14:1). What business does the spiritually wise have communing with the natural fool? The fool is proud, knowing nothing, but is obsessed with disputes and arguments over words, from which come envy, strife, reviling, evil suspicions and constant friction of men of corrupt minds and destitute of the truth… (1 Timothy 6:4-5).

Now there are some people who do have the Spirit of God, but have not yet been led to the truth, for I was once among them. I call them borderline believers or non-believers. In such cases, when you speak to them about the truth, they will listen with an open mind and heart, ready to soak up the Word of God that lies dormant within them. Although they will ask valid questions about our faith and spiritual matters, they do not stop up their ears and trample over what we say. It is peoples such as these that we believers must snatch out of the fire, because they are our God's chosen children, though they do not yet know it.

A prime example of when I found myself kicking dead horses took place in 2014. I was debating with a natural man on a popular social media website. The natural man scoffed at me for reading a bible that had been doctored and revised so many times, that the truth was obscured. I assured the natural man that my faith and belief came not from the bible, but the God of Creation Himself, through Jesus Christ whom I had an intimate relationship and was in constant communication with. I added that although the bible had been translated and re-written by imperfect men, I still considered it to be a useful guide. The natural man became angry that my spiritual insight came from a higher source other than the bible, so he moved on to his next attack, stating, "Sista, I can't believe that your black ass is worshiping a white God! You should be ashamed." At this, I told the natural man that no one alive has seen the face of the Son of God, and therefore no one knows the color of His skin which the bible describes as bronze.

I also added that no matter what shade of skin the Lord Jesus Christ has, it did not make a difference to me. At the end of the day, He died so that we could all live (regardless of out race/ethnicity), and that was all that mattered to me. Frustrated that he could not diminish my faith and belief in the Son of God, the natural man tried introducing me to a new doctrine, stating, "We humans are all gods. We all have power, but some of us are ignorant and haven't tapped into it, like you." By this time, I was increasingly growing tired of the natural man's lies. I saw that he could not win a debate through wisdom and knowledge and was now resorting to blatantly insulting me. I decided to close the debate with the natural man by challenging his belief that he was some sort of god. I asked, "How come you did not create yourself if you are truly a god? How did you create your parents? If you are truly a god, then surely you would never get sick or die. Why would you allow your friends and family to pass away instead of healing them? Why do you work if you are a god? Shouldn't you be able to snap your fingers or twinkle your nose and anything you wish for will appear? Why do you have problems in your life if you are a god? You have met people who told you about places that you have never been to and you believe them. People have also told you about God and Jesus Christ. Why don't you believe them too?" Rather than recognizing the error in his thinking, the natural man started to hurl insults at me without addressing the validity of my questions.

Another time I found myself guilty of kicking dead horses and casting my pearls before swine took place when I found myself in a heated debate with a loved one. In the past, I would always argue harder with those closest to me because I wanted the best for them. In short, as I was relaying the Word of God to this person over the phone, he abruptly cut me off and began shouting over me, "You're crazy! You're crazy!" repeatedly until I stopped speaking. I was really hurt by his response because I loved this person who was devaluing my beliefs. I could not understand why we could not have a difference of opinion without verbally abusing one another. Needless to say, that was the last time I tried to relay the mysteries of God to someone who had no spiritual understanding whatsoever. It was also the last time I would ever be guilty of kicking a dead horse again.

Have you ever heard of the television series called, *The Walking Dead*? Well, that is the best way to describe the non-believer who walks around in the natural, but is dead in spirit. The only way for the spirit to live is through Christ Jesus. Do not be delusional. We are not gods, but rather we were created by God. I address this letter to believers in Jesus not to prevent them from spreading the Gospel of Truth to non-believers- to the contrary, warn them, but do not spend precious time in these last days engaged in fruitless debates. Questions and concerns about my faith are encouraged, but I refuse to argue or debate about it. Anytime a conversation turns negative or argumentative, I quickly disengage as I have no time or energy to fuel stupidity, nor do I feel the need to prove anything to anyone, but God. We must realize that some people, as open minded as they claim to be, just don't want to hear or except certain truths. This does not mean that they never will, but they are not ready now. Do not give to dogs what is Holy, and do not throw your pearls before swine, or they will trample them under their feet, and turn to tear you to pieces (Matthew 7:6). Many of you can also bear witness to this truth. Let's stop kicking dead horses.

Distractions

After listening to Dr. Tony Evans' sermon about stagnation in the lives of Christians last night, I was motivated to cover the topic of distractions. Listening to Evans made me reflect on the distractions that have been placed in my path both by others and by myself. I say myself as well because I know that my obnoxious vices and disobedience to Jesus Christ hinders me and blocks me from living up to my full potential. Knowing that the enemy's goal is to distract me, you would think that I would be on guard, but while my mind and spirit is fixed on the Lord, my sinful flesh craves worldly things. I have noticed that the more I seek after the God of Creation, the more obstacles and distractions are put in my way. The closer I come to reaching my spiritual goals, the more

"Big brother isn't watching. He's sing and dancing. He's pulling rabbits out of a hat. Big brother's busy holding your attention every moment you're awake, he's making sure you're always distracted. He's making sure you're fully absorbed."
-Chuck Palahniuk

opposition I come up against.

Our enemy is very crafty. Do you really thing that Satan wants us to get to know God? Try picking up a bible and see if the phone rings, or the baby wakes up, or the kids start running amuck, or you realize it's time to prepare dinner, or you have to go to work- anything to distract us from our walk with Jesus Christ. Then there are the plans we make to go to church or study the bible, but things seem to keep coming up. We have to work overtime that day, we have to drop the kids off at basketball practice or clean the house. All of these things that arise is no coincidence, but the devil's way of keeping us distracted enough, that we have no time to develop a relationship with our Lord and Savior.

The beauty of it all is that we don't have to feel guilty about all of our broken promises to get to know God. The excuses we think we have made are not really excuses, but actual distractions designed to throw us off our spiritual course. It is the devil's job to spiritually distract us, and we all know, he does a fine job at it. Spiritual distractions are intentional and can come in many forms and at any time. Distractions from our children, discord in the family and problems at work are just a few external distractions. Other times, we can distract and oppress ourselves with alcohol, drugs,

"If we let ourselves, we shall always be waiting for some distraction or other end before we can really get down to our work. The only people who achieve much are those who want knowledge so badly that they seek it while conditions are still unfavorable. Favorable conditions never come."
-C.S. Lewis

"Most people are so absorbed in the contemplation of the outside world that they are wholly oblivious to what is passing on within themselves." -Nikola Tesla

gambling, sex and other vices. Anything that goes against the will of the God of Creation hinders our spiritual growth. We become spiritually stagnated and do not know why. We have all been guilty of letting distractions get in the way of our progress in some way or another.

It is important to keep our eyes open for the enemy's snares and distractions so that our feet will stumble a little less often. The key to overcoming distractions is to be deliberate. We must deliberately find time or make time for our Lord and Savior, in spite of the things that will surely come against us when we seek God. On the occasion that we do fall, we must rise again, dust off our clothes, lick our wounds if we must, but move forward still. Following Christ is not always easy with all that Satan does to distract us, but if we can at least try, God will see and have mercy on us. Thank the Lord that we are saved by mercy and grace and not by our works (Ephesians 2:8-9). Amen

Betrayal

As a child of God, I could literally testify for weeks on end about those who have betray me. I could go on and on about those who have poisoned my food, threatened me, tried to lead me astray, or used witchcraft against me and my children without cause. I could testify about people who have come into my home with smiles to cover up their ill intentions; who have unloaded their negative energy upon me; who have tried to drain me of my energy; who have slandered my name for the sake of the Name. I honestly feel that I know more about betrayal than anyone, but Christ Jesus Himself. Back in the day, the way I would have handled disrespect or betrayal was with a tongue lashing and an iron fist. I used to take pride in my independence and strong willed nature. But when

"Lord protect me from my friends, I can take care of my enemies."
-Voltaire

"Be wary of friends. They will betray you more quickly, for they are easily aroused to envy."
-Robert Greene

"Wishing to be friends is quick work, but friendship is a slow ripening fruit."
-Aristotle

"Thus for my own part I have been deceived by the person I loved most and of whose love, above everyone else's, I have been most confident."
-Baldassare Castiglione

Jesus Christ took over my life, I found it a strange sensation not to fight my own battles, but to let God do it for me.

There are many people who hold a grudge against God and hate Him with a passion. The fact that Christ chose to reveal Himself in me really brought out their wickedness, and they fiercely stood against me, taking out all of their animosity towards Him on me. Granted, I expect no one to love and worship the Lord as I do, but if do not enter your home with malicious intent, then I expect the same courtesy in return. Frankly, I'm not phony enough to pretend friendship when I truly dislike someone. It's deceitful and takes too much effort on my part. Also, God looks at the heart, and I refuse to be another Judas Iscariot. During the hardest time in my life, both family and friends ploted on me behind my back and treated me horribly. I sat back and watched friends and relatives who never hung out or had anything in common, suddenly come together to destroy me. I felt like I was trapped in a never ending episode of *Survivor* because love ones became my enemies, uniting to thwart me. They respected nothing, which is why we are no longer friends. My new family and friends are those who are in Christ.

I never understood how I could enter someone's house feeling healthy, vivacious and energetic, but leave it feeling completely drained, lame and physically ill. I skipped happily into a home, but left it in excruciating pain and limping terribly. There was also those who entertained lying familiar spirits and would allow ungodly spirits to use them at will. They would often make the most bizarre statements out of the clear blue, mostly about keeping my mouth shut. Because Jesus Christ was operating in my life, I allowed some people to come in and out of my life through the power of forgiveness, only to be bitten by the same snake time and time again.

There was one who treated me so badly, that I almost lost all faith and trust in humanity, but not in Jesus. When I chose Christ, this woman really made my life a living hell. She became so wicked that things would mysteriously go wrong anytime she was present. My television reception would grow faint and staticy, the internet would go out and lights would start flickering when she was around. I always felt physically drained and my body would ache during and after her unwanted visits. Simply put, she was bad news. Her mere presence brought arguing, fighting, discord amongst my

"This is the fate that faces all of us when we sympathize with our enemies, when pity or the hope of reconciliation makes us pull back from doing away with them. We only strengthen their fear and hatred of us... yet we nurture these resentful vipers who will one day kill us."
-Robert Greene

"A lot of people let me down... A lot of the people I thought were my friends turned on me."
-Lil' Kim

"My attitude towards friendship has remained the same. I will support you with all the love in my heart, but if it's not reciprocal, I gotta go..."
-RuPaul

children and I and turmoil in my home. When I tell you things went wrong when she was there, I mean it.

When I dislike a person, I stay far away from them, but there are some who will go out of their way to relentlessly pursue those they hate. One particular time, I was in my bedroom working on a book when the enemy sent this person aknocking. Since I do not allow visitors to just come over without calling first, I ignored the door. The knocking became so loud and persistent that I believed it was the police. As I exited my room and walked to the door, I heard the woman's voice calling out to me, so I sat back down. I had long ago tired of her tricks and decided to distance myself from her. After pounding at the door and calling out to me for several more minutes, it was silent and I assumed she had finally given up and left. Five minutes passed when I heard bashing and crashing noises in my living room. When I ran out of my bedroom and into my living room, I found her standing in my living room looking angry. Looking past her, I saw that she had kicked my back door down, splintering the wood and rendering the lock completely useless. I lived on the second floor of an apartment building, so how she managed to access the second floor balcony to kick my door down, I will leave to your imaginations. I assumed she flew up on her broom.

"I know damn well you heard me knocking," she barked.

"Well, maybe I didn't want to be bothered! I'm not obligated to have visitors in my home if I don't want any," I hollered, irritated that she would go so far to gain access to someone's house that she did not even like or get along with anyway.

I walked over to the back door and tried to close and lock it, but it would not even shut all of the way.

"You actually broke my door down knowing that I live in a bad neighborhood and my children have to sleep here?" I asked her in disgust.

The woman just rolled her eyes at me. "I'm sorry," she halfheartedly offered.

"Get out!" I ordered as I walked back to my bedroom.

I knew that one of the enemy's devices was distraction. Had I been smoking weed or watching television, all would have been well, but the moment I was working on something positive like job hunting or book writing, the enemy would use someone or something to distract me. As I started to pick up on my book where I left off, my computer mysteriously went haywire and shut off. I turned around to see the unwanted visitor standing behind me staring at the computer screen. Once again, I ordered the pesky visitor to leave my house, but in response, she kicked off her shoes and began to put her feet in my shoes that were on the floor. She was slipping into a second pair of shoes by the time arose to literally escort her out of my bedroom and out of the door. As soon as she was gone, I threw out the shoes she put on. I was so tired of people who did not even like me, coming around me with the same old shenanigans. I was sickened by the feelings they left me with; tearing at my spirit and leaving me in agony and pain. I know that scripture tells us, "We wrestle not against flesh and blood, but against spiritual wickedness (Ephesians 6:12), but I did not think it was fun, though it may be true. I knew that not one of the people who came against me could ever beat me in the physical, so they fought me in spirit, which was not fair. Looking back at it now, I never knew anyone of them to fight fair, so I cannot blame them for following their corrupt hearts. The bible also says: "And ye shall be betrayed by both parents and brethren and kinfolks and friends; and some of you they shall cause to be put to death (not the soul, but the body) (Luke 21:16).

Basically, I have been betrayed by many on all levels. The gifts that the God of Creation had bestow upon me were being selfishly misused. They did not want God, but they wanted what He could give. I saw that because I had chosen Christ, that I was hated by friends, family and my fiancé (who was so wicked and cruel, that he needs a chapter to himself), without cause. In return for my love, they became my accusers. They rewarded me evil for good and hatred for my love (Psalm 109:4-5) without shame. Whenever they were sick, I prayed for them; whenever they were hungry, I fed them; when they were broke, I lent them money; when they needed a place to go to escape crazy lovers, my door was always open to them. But in my adversity, they rejoiced and gathered together; attackers gathered against me and I did not know it; they tore at me and did not cease (Psalm 35:15). During this time, I felt like a lamb among hungry, hateful, jealous lions. They surrounded me with smiles, tearing me to pieces and plotting my demise all the while. Though I felt resentment, I never felt helpless because my help comes from the Lord, the Maker of heaven and earth. During this time, I had fashioned myself as some sort of guinea pig that the Lord uses to test the hearts of men and women who came in contact with me. Perhaps God wanted to see who was for Him and whom was against Him, through me. Unfortunately, I can testify that more people that I knew where against Him, and few were for Him.

The things I have told you about do not even touch the tip of the iceberg of all that I have been through in the valley. Many things that have also become part of my testimony in Christ Jesus, I have left out because the memory of them are so painful. If some people had gone through what I have been through and saw what my eyes have seen, many might have lost their minds, committed suicide or just be driven plain mad. In this respect, I thank the Lord God Almighty that He has kept my mind sound and preserved me. Despite the fact that many betray me and stabbed me in the back, I feel bad for them. For God has revealed to me their destinies, if they do not confess and repent of their sins and turn from their wicked ways. Also, although it was not an easy time in my life, I took heart that I did have a few loyal friends and relatives who knew I loved Christ and still, they did nothing to harm me, shun me or mistreat me. I pray for them a bit more frequently than I pray for my enemy's, and have no doubt at all that I will see them in the Kingdom of God in the second life which is forever, Amen. It's kind of like the two thieves who were hanging on the cross beside Christ. Though both were guilty of sin, one thief blasphemed and mocked Christ, while the other thief did nothing against Him. The thief may not have been innocent of sin, yet did nothing to harm Christ and did not insult Him, joined Him in the Paradise that very day (Luke 23:33-43).

It might have been easy to cut off friends that betray me, but it was difficult to turn away from my own blood relatives. I held my family to a higher standard of loyalty, but in the end, they hurt me the most. I was not until they began to involve my children (my most precious asset in this dark world) that I realized that I had to sever ties with them, as much as I loved them. They were planting seeds that I was a bad mother and doing whatever they could to promote fighting and discord between my children and I. I was not willing to sacrifice the relationship and tight knit bond that I have always had with my babies. Unless those who betray me confesses and repents, I will forever keep my distance from them. Only Jesus Christ Himself can change their hearts and renew the right spirit within them. Until then, I will let the wicked dig their own graves, without my involvement.

Rather than become bitter about all I have endured at the hands of my loved ones, I look back at their evil deeds and feel pity towards them. I ask our Heavenly Father to forgive them for they know not what they do. I also thank them from the bottom of my heart for helping to strengthen my testimony for Christ. That said, I also will not hesitate to testify against them when the time comes, if they refuse to repent. After everything that I have endured from them in the first life, would it be fair to be forced to endure the same people in the second life also? Certainly not!

Jealousy

As God is my witness, I truly believe that jealousy (as I have always warned my children) is the most the dangerous of all human emotion. Jealous, goes hand in hand with its partner envy, and can drive a person to commit every kind of evil towards their neighbor from ill wishing to plotting murder. There is absolutely nothing under the sun that a jealous person isn't capable of doing. There is no line they are unwilling to cross, for where jealousy, envy and self-seeking exists, confusion and everything are there (James 3:16). In walking with Christ, I have seen people who were actually jealous of my intimate relationship with God. Rather than pursue their own relationships with Christ Jesus and our Heavenly Father, they found it more convenient to

"From a little spark, may burst a flame."
-Dante Alighieri

conspire, plot and slander me. A jealous person lusts and does not have. They murder and covet and still cannot obtain. They fight and war and still have nothing because they do not ask God for what they seek (James 4:2). A jealous person puts too much focus on what others have and what others are doing to improve their own condition. In contrast, some people can have more than you have, and still be jealous of you.

Jealousy is a spirit (Numbers 5:14), and we all know where the spirit of jealousy comes from- the devil. Has Satan not shown us his jealous nature from the beginning? In the day when the sons of man came to present themselves before the Lord, Satan the accuser also came among them. It was at that time that Satan first accused Job of not fearing God, not out of love and respect, but for profit and selfish gain (Job 1:6-12). Believe it or not, the ways of the devil have not changed from the time of old, but have only worsened, for he knows that he has but a short time to deceive and test us. On judgement day, the accuser will undoubtedly be present to recant all of our sins before our Lord and accuse us of not being worthy to enter into the Kingdom of God, and why? It is simply because Satan is jealous of you. He hates your guts because you are made in the image of the One True Living God and His Holy Son. Satan does not have the power to destroy God, but he does have the power to destroy you by taking your soul to hell, but only if you let him. It was Satan's jealous spirit that made him want to go to war with God in the first place, therefore, never under estimate anyone with this spirit. Sever any ties you may have with such a person and closely watch those who you suspect are secretly jealous of you. After all, what benefit is there in pursuing a relationship of any kind with persons with a jealous spirit? Sure a jealous person can display a few good qualities, but so does the devil appear to be angelic. At the end of the day, such a relationship will prove to be toxic and your own undoing.

Forgiveness (Vengeance Is Mine)

I used to have violent thoughts about getting revenge on those who wronged me. I would be so upset, that I imagined running them down with my car. For the life of me, I could not understand how people could be so unloyal to someone who would have died to save them as Christ would have and did. Then I remembered what Christ Himself said on the cross of Calvary: "Forgive them Father, for they know not what they do (Luke 23:34)." And if Jesus Christ forgave, then who am I to hold a grudge? Do we ask our Heavenly Father to forgive us our sins and trespasses, but not the sins and trespasses of others? Also, allow me to digress by telling you that I would never truly harm my neighbors despite the wicked thoughts of vengeance I once held. Plus, Genghis Khan warned us that action committed in anger is doomed to failure and I do

"True forgiveness is when you can say, "Thank you for that experience." -Oprah Winfrey

"I have always found that mercy bears richer fruits than strict justice." Abraham Lincoln

not want to go to jail, lest my enemies will rejoice. I will not repay evil for evil or insult with insult (Peter 3:9 & Romans 12:17). It was God's sovereign Word which I knew to be faithful and true that prevented me from going off the deep end.

I think of all of the mistakes I have made and wrongs I had committed (not against my neighbor, but against God and myself) that Christ has forgiven me for, though I am not worthy. I keep in mind that if we forgive other people when they sin against us, then our Heavenly Father will also forgive us. But if we do not forgive others their sins, our Father will not forgive us our sins (Matthew 6:14-15). In addition to that, holding such animosity in my heart was darkening me and making me physically sick. I knew that in order to move forward, I had to rid myself of all bitterness, rage, anger, brawling and slander along with every form of malice (Ephesians 4:31). I took comfort in the fact that I serve a just God who would not let my enemy's wickedness go unpunished. Even if their punishment was not as swift as I would have liked, it would still take place in His timing as He says: "Never take our own revenge, beloved, but leave room for the wrath of God, for it is written, "Vengeance is mine, I will repay," says the Lord. But if your enemy is hungry, feed him, and if he is thirsty, give him a drink; for in doing so you will reap burning coals on his head (Romans 12: 19-20).

Forgiving someone who has hurt us so deeply is never easy ladies and gentleman, but it is necessary. We do this not for those who have wronged us, but for ourselves and for the God of Creation. We also need to recognize that unhealthy, unproductive thoughts of vengeance and destruction come from Satan himself. It is only when we can forgive, rebuking all negative thoughts and take up the armor of God that we can truly move forward with our lives.

Letting Go

After forgiveness, letting go is the next phase of the healing process. It takes great character and an open heart to truly let go of the pain that someone has caused you. For most of us, time heals all wounds, but for some people, time only gives the wound time to fester and become ugly. I used to be one that held a mean grudge, but when God is truly operating in your life, you learn to let go and have faith that He will avenge and redeem you.

As time has gone by and old wounds have healed and new wounds are starting to, I've been finding it easier and easier to forgive those who have let me down or disappointed me. I even pray for my enemies just as fervently as I pray for the few loyal friends and family that remain in my life. This is why I was so perplexed

"Resentment is like drinking poison and then hoping it will kill your enemies."
-Nelson Mandela

"Forgiveness is not about forgetting. It is about letting go of another person's throat… Forgiveness does not create a relationship. Unless people speak the truth about what they have done and change their mind and behavior, a relationship is not possible. Forgiveness in no way requires that you trust the one you forgive."
-William Paul Young

when a friend of mine recently accused me of not 'letting go'. Now, before you gather the rocks to stone me, allow me to paint a picture for you…

A former friend tried to reach out to me after betraying me in the worst way. Although I had forgiven this person in my heart and before our Heavenly Father in prayer, I declined their offer to hang out and break bread together. I feel that just because I have forgiven someone, I was under no obligation to commune with them. Also, the betrayal was so unwarranted that I could never trust that person anymore. In any case, not everyone is destined to walk this walk with me. Some people are in our lives for a lifetime, some for years, some for a season and some for the time being. So as I'm relating this information to my friend over a glass of wine, I spoke of this person's constant attempts to reach out to me.

"You need to let go of the past." My friend said, then suggested that I rekindle the friendship.

Just to find out how far he would go with his 'letting go of the past theory', I inquired of my former boss who constantly tried to get me fired and even made a false call to Child Protective Services to accuse me of child abuse. Then I asked about the trusted platonic friend who tried to rape me after a few drinks at his place.

"And what of them? Should I call the two of them up and invite them over for dinner and a movie since I forgave them in my heart and before God, too?" I challenged.

My friend sat there twiddling his thumbs for a moment and was at a loss for words, just as I suspected he would be. I figured that I had made my point that by forgiving, I was letting go. Going backwards however, was simply not in my nature unless Christ Himself directed me to do so. I learned the hard way the price paid for forgiving someone and later reacquainting myself with them.

Just as I rose to refresh our drinks, my friend said to me, "Sometimes when people bring up the past, it can be hurtful, especially when we know we've done something wrong. We don't need anyone throwing it up in our faces."

I thought about what he said and agreed with him, after all, have we not all fallen short of God's glory? Never the less, all of my hardships and experiences in the valley has given unto me a testimony in Jesus Christ that cannot be denied. I do not have amnesia, nor did I bump my head and forget all I have been through, even though I have forgiven my trespassers and let go of all ungodly feelings towards them.

A Call to Endure

Being persecuted in this world for your love of Jesus Christ is not easy, but the rewards are there if you can endure it. I never imagined that months after graduating college, that I would be a single mother with two teenaged kids sleeping in a Dodge Neon for the sake of the Name. I stood back and watched people that I loved dearly begin to separate themselves from me. I have already spoken to you about the family and friends who formerly shared little in common forging alliances against me. I have always believed that you reap what you sow, but sometimes in life, we reap what we have not sown. If I had ever lifted my hand to harm, opened my mouth to slander or wished ill upon you, then whatever negativity befalls me, so be it deservingly. I loved and was loyal to those who became my enemies, not for anything that I had done to them, but

"I love those who can smile in trouble, who can gather strength from distress, and grow brave by reflection. 'Tis the business of little minds to shrink, but they whose heart is firm, and whose conscious approves their conduct, will pursue their principles unto death." - Leonardo da Vinci

simply because I love Christ.
The world shall hate you because they hated our Heavenly Father and his son (John 15:18). Minus the sores and boils, I felt as if I were experiencing the trials of Job. I remembered reading about how Satan constantly approached the God of creation claiming that if He took away all that Job had, that Job would turn and curse God's holy name (Job 1:11). I figured that maybe Satan was doing the same concerning me. Folks, when I tell you that I lost everything, I really mean it. My lover turned on me and threw my children and I out on the streets, my dad and I grew distant, and it seemed like my sisters and brothers were always mad at me for some reason or another. Everyone, including strangers lined up to use and exploit me for the gifts that God had given me. Almost everywhere I went, I could feel the anger and resentment people felt because Christ was wit me. Employers looked down on me with distain, refusing me work. For quite some time, I wandered from place to place with my children without a stable place to call home where I might rest. People on the street would whisper and speculate about me in passing as if I could not hear them. Although the world made me feel like an outcast, I did not care. I was born poor and I

"All that was great in the past was ridiculed, condemned, combatted, suppressed- only to emerge all the more powerfully, all the more triumphantly from the struggle."
-Nikola Tesla

"In my country we go to prison first and then become president."
-Nelson Mandela

"It is easier to find men who will volunteer to die, than to find those who are willing to endure pain with patience."
-Julius Caesar

grew up in a tumultuous household, so I was used to hardships. The fact that I was a shy child prepared me for a life of solitude. Back in the day when I was stripping, getting high and making merry, the world loved me, but when I gave my life to Jesus Christ, the world hated me. The only reason that I am sharing my testimony with all of you is because I want to warn you of what you may endure for Christ's sake. These things they will do to you because they have not known the Father nor the Son (John 16:3). I tell you that the more good you do (or are), the more evil you will attract. Satan would never pick on those who are doing his will. Those who will hate you are in darkness and hate the light because they cannot hide in the light, lest they will be exposed.

Now that I have made peace with the past and moved on in love and forgiveness, I can hold my head up high and share my testimony with you. I plead with you to endure the persecutions, hardships and strongholds for the Son of Man. If I had looked forward to worldly rewards, I would have joined the long list of those who have sold themselves to this world long ago. Instead, I look not to what is temporal, but what is eternal (2 Corinthians 4:18) and everlasting, which is the Kingdom of God. I have resolved that if I have to live out the rest of my short life on earth in strife, then so be it. I do not love this dark world or anything in it, but I do love people, regardless of how they feel about me. It's rather peculiar to love even those who despise you. I do not want to scare you with my tales of woe and suffering for Jesus Christ. My aim is only to warn you that the worldly *people of this world will try to break you*, and they will be relentless in their quest. Pray for courage and stand strong in the faith. Be ready to endure any obstacles, trials, tribulations, persecution and forces of darkness that may come against you during your walk with Jesus Christ. For I consider that the sufferings of this present time are not worthy to be compared with the glory which shall be revealed in us (Romans 8:18).

In closing, I want you to think about the pursuit of the Kingdom of God as the ultimate game of survival of the fittest. To win, we must be sober and vigilant because our adversary the devil walks about like a roaring lion, seeking whom he may devour. Resist him (and his puppets), knowing that the same sufferings are also experienced by your brotherhood in the world (Peter 5:8-9) and you are not alone in the fight. I warn you in advance that all who desire to live godly in Christ will suffer persecution (2 Timothy 3:12), but he who endures to the end shall be saved (Mark 13:13). The books of Matthew and Revelations also warn us of the persecution that will come from the men of this world, but do not fear man who can kill the body and after that do no more. Rather fear God who can destroy both body and soul in hell (Matthew 10:28). Also, take comfort that though the world may hate you, our Heavenly Father promises us that if we believe in Him and His Son, not a hair on our head should be lost (Luke 21:18), nor will the plagues, famine and disasters described in the book of Revelations affect us who have endured for Christ's sake.

Faith Is the Key

By definition, faith is the confidence, belief or trust in someone or something, but it is also the assurance of things hoped for and the conviction of things not seen (Hebrews 11:1). Faith, in combination with hope, is the key to our salvation in Jesus Christ, friends. Without faith, it is impossible to please God because you must believe that He exists in order to receive His rewards (Hebrews 11:6). It is also what sets the believer apart from the non-believer. But here is the kicker: If there is a shed of doubt- even a hint, your faith is made null and void. Did our Lord and savior Jesus Christ not tell us, "Assuredly, I say to you, if you have faith and do not doubt, you will not only do what was done to the fig tree, but also if you say to this mountain, 'Be removed

"There are no tricks in plain and simple faith."
-Julius Caesar

"One cannot prepare for something while secretly believing it will not happen."
-Nelson Mandela

and cast into the sea,' it will be done. And whatever things you ask in prayer, believing, you will receive (Matthew 21:21-22)."

One of my favorite bible illustrations about faith and doubt is found in the book of Matthews. Jesus was walking on water in the midst of a great storm when he called out to Peter to come to Him. Peter leaves the boat and begins to walk on the water to meet the Lord, but when he saw how strong the winds were, he became afraid and began to sink, crying out, "Lord save me!" Immediately Jesus stretched out His hand and caught Peter, saying, "O you of little faith, why did you doubt?" We see that it was Peter's faith that allowed him to walk on water and his doubt that caused him to sink. We also see that if our faith starts to wane, we can still call on the name of the Lord and be saved.

Works alone is simply not enough to please God, but faith is the key (Ephesians 2:8-9). I have always been good to my neighbors; always generous in giving, gifting and loaning to the poor and needy. I have never held back in helping my brothers and sisters when they needed me, keeping my door open to those who fell on hard times. I also know many other people who have done the same unto their neighbor. Despite this, I realized that it was never my works alone, but my unshakeable faith in the God of Creation and His Holy Son that I was saved by His mercy and His grace. Rehab may have been a common prostitute, but she had enough faith and common sense to hide the Lord's spies, who later spared the lives of her and her family. We do not need a quantity of faith, but if we have faith as small as a mustard seed, we too shall be saved (Matthew 11:20). So have faith friends, without doubting. For the one who doubts is like a wave of the sea that is driven and tossed by the wind. For that person must not suppose that he will receive anything from the Lord; he is a double-minded man, unstable in all his ways (James 1:6-8).

And if you see a brother or sister with little faith, do not look down on them, but rather lift them up (Luke22:32) because we are all responsible for one another.

There's Hope

Hope is the one thing that costs you nothing and can never be taken away from you. Every day that you wake up, until you take your last breath, there's still hope. I charge all of you to consider each day that you wake up as a second chance at life; a second chance for all of us to do a little bit better than we did the day before. Some people did not wake up to see this day, but for some reason or another, the God of Creation woke you up and preserved you. Let us all be grateful and dare I say thankful to the Lord Almighty, for everyday His mercies are new (Lamentations 3:22-23).

Hope is precious. Hold onto hope with both of your hands. Bind her and chain her around your heart if you must, but never let hope go. Be sure

"Hold fast to dreams,
For if dreams die
Life is like a broken-winged bird,
That cannot fly."
-Langston Hughes

to steer clear of doubters and naysayers who will try to destroy your hopes. Remember that hope goes hand in hand with faith and love and are the keys to our salvation in Christ Jesus. And for in this hope we are saved (Romans8:24).

Stop Worrying

People **always ask me** directly or indirectly, if I fear death or being hurt by someone because of my faith in Jesus Christ. They bring up other figures who stood in their truths like Martin Luther King Jr., John F. Kennedy, William Cooper and even Jesus Christ himself who all came to their demises because they loved the truth in a dark world full of corrupt minded people. I see the concern in their eyes and say to them, "Stop worrying."

Truth be told, I have lost so much for Christ's sake, until nothing in this world matters to me anymore. The only thing I truly fear is hell. Besides, I feel that when I cry or lament over what I cannot help, I look wicked in the eyes of the Lord for not trusting Him. Worrying shows the Lord that we do not trust that He will make things better or turn things around for

"The wise man does not expose himself needlessly to danger, since there are few things for which he cares sufficiently; but he is willing, in great crises, to give even his life- knowing that under certain conditions it is not worthwhile to live."
-Aristotle

our good and His glory To worry means that doubt lies within our heart, which cancels out our hope and faith in Him. To worry is to be fearful and God is love.

On this journey, I have learned that both in happiness and hardships, to trust in the Lord. He is our helper. As much as I have some concerns about the future, I have made the conscious choice not to worry about it. Instead, I cast all fear, worry and anxiety on the Lord because He cares for us. When we stop worrying, we show God that we truly and fully trust in Him to make provisions for us, and His provisions are sufficient. To worry is not to believe. We trust too much in what we can do for ourselves or what others can do for us when we should rely on God, the giver of life. If He created us, He will be faithful to provide for us and uphold us.

So should I fear death as a follower of Christ? Absolutely not! If someone was to kill my body, my soul would go to Paradise, so why would I fear that? Not only do I like the idea of heaven but I spend my life looking forward to it. In any case, when we hurt our neighbors and do not repent, we only damn ourselves. Besides, only the Heavenly Father knows when our short time is finished on this earth, so what's the use of worrying? Can any one of you extend his life another day or hour by worrying (Matthew 6:27 & Luke 12:25)? Please stop worrying about me or yourselves, because that's God's job, and He does not need anyone's help to do His work.

"There comes a time when one must take a position that is neither safe, nor politic, nor popular, but he must take it because his conscience tells him it is right."
-Martin Luther King Jr.

Why Our Father Sent His Son

How many of us would have been **willing** to send our only son to be delivered into people's filthy hands; to become a pure living sacrifice to atone for the sins of the world, as our Heavenly Father did? That was just one of the ways that the God of Creation shows us how much He loves us and how compassionate He is towards us. I think that it is unfortunate that so many people have the wrong impression concerning their maker. To be honest, I am not sure how Satan has managed to project *his* true nature and image onto our Lord and savior, but he has. The devil has made the blind hate God, but God is our friend, not our enemy. People think that the God of Creation sits on high with malice and ill intent, ready to judge and condemn them to hell,

"…He does not expect his ideas will be readily taken up. His work is like that of a planter- for the future. His duty is to lay up the foundation for those who are to come, and point the way."
-Nikola Tesla

but that is not the will of God to destroy, but it is the will of Satan who comes to kill and destroy (John 10:10). So, the next time when the devil tries to plant the seed of deception about our Christ, recognize that the seed has been planted by the Father of Lies. The thief comes to steal, kill and destroy, but Jesus has come so that we may have life. While the devil stands in front of God to accuse men (as he is called the accuser), Jesus intercedes for us on our behalf. Satan is the prosecutor, and Jesus Christ the defender of men.

One of the main reasons that God sent His Son was so that we would not have to die a second death, but can live eternally in His Heavenly Kingdom. For God so loved the world that He gave His only begotten Son, that whoever believe in Him should not perish, but have everlasting life. For God did not send His Son into the world to condemn the world, but that through Him we might be saved (John 3:1617). Jesus Himself tells us, "I am the way, the truth and the life. No one comes to the Father except through me (John 14:6).

Jesus is not called the Good Shepard simply because it's cutesy, but because He was willing to lay down His life for His sheep (us) (Matthew 18:11-14). What's ironic is that those who sought to crucify Christ Jesus only fooled themselves into thinking that they had taken His life, but in actuality, Christ lay down His life voluntarily (John 10:18-19), and also took it up again by the power that was granted to Him from His Father.

Repent and Be Baptized

Since we know not the day or hour
of the return of Jesus Christ, we need
to repent of our sins and be baptized
today, before it is too late. Many of
you have been straddling the fence for
far too long and must make a choice
and take a stance for or against Christ
now. Yes, we have all sinned, but we
are not all bad people, deserving of
hell. The time is now that we should
come to our senses and escape the
snare of the devil who has taken us
captive to do his will for far too long.
Let not your understanding be
darkened, your hearts blinded,
alienated from the God of Creation
who loves you and waits to redeem
you from your sins.

    This is how to be saved and enter
into the Kingdom of God: "Confess
with your mouths the Lord Jesus and
believe that God has raised Him from
the dead, and you will be saved. For

"Bad men are
full of
repentance."
-Aristotle

"There is an
afterlife. I am
convinced of
this."
-Paulo Coelho

"While I
thought I was
learning how to
live; I have
been learning
how to die."
-Leonardo da
Vinci

with the heart, one believes unto righteousness and with the mouth confession is made unto salvation. For the Scripture says, "Whoever believes in Him will not be put to shame." There is no distinction between Greek and Jew, for the same Lord over all is rich to all who call upon Him (Romans 10:9-12). How I wish I could be with you all now! I would literally get down on my hands and knees before you and plead with you to repent and be baptized (because there is absolutely no shame in my game). I promise you that unless you repent of your sins, you will all likewise perish (Luke 13:3). Save yourselves friends. Save your children and your spouse. Save your kinfolks and your friends. Between you and I, I confess my sins to the Lord Almighty every week, but recently I have decided that I wanted to be re-baptized as a symbol of my rededication to Christ Jesus. Please confess your sins and be baptized with me.

My Weekly Prayer of Confession and Repentance:

Father God,

I humbly come before you to confess my sins of (state your sins). Lord, I need you to forgive me and cleanse me of my sins, in the name of Jesus Heavenly Father, I know that anyone who calls on your name will be saved, and anyone who comes to you for forgiveness will be forgiven. I fully believe in your Word and rely on your promise for I know that you cannot lie. Please forgive me and have mercy on my soul, Lord Jesus. Renew the right spirit within me, Lord. My heart and my intentions are good, but my flesh is weak. Give me the strength to fight off the devil and do your Holy will. I do not want to go to hell, and I know that only you can save me from the second death. Walk with me Lord Jesus and hold my hand so I will not be led astray. In the name of Jesus, I pray. Amen

Many of You Belong to God & Don't Know It... Yet

Many of you belong to God and don't even know it
...yet. Yes, even *you* wicked people. Need I remind you of
the story of Saul of Tarsus, who became the apostle Paul?
Saul hated the God of Creation and relentlessly pursued
followers of Jesus Christ to persecute, jail and murder them. It
was not until Christ revealed Himself to Saul that Saul finally
came to his senses and began to serve and worship the One
True Living God. The apostle Paul is not the only one who
has this testimony. Former Satanist and occultist around the
world also share their testimonies of how they came to know
and love Christ Jesus, as well. It is a powerful experience
when the veil is lifted and the scales that blind us fall from
our eyes. There is no greater revelation in the world than the
revelation of the Son of Man's existence. The experience is
not only extraordinary, but life changing.

   In reality we are not fully in control of our destinies, but
the God of Creation is. We know not what tomorrow will
bring, let alone if we will live to see it, but He knows. Those
who prematurely condemn themselves to hell because of

their sins will actually spend their eternal lives in the Paradise of the Kingdom of God. For whom He foreknew, He also predestined to be conformed to the image of His Son (Jesus Christ), that he might be the firstborn among many brethren (Romans 8:29). Did you know that the God of Creation calls upon the worst of sinners to serve Him? Heck, look at Saul or even myself. He chose us not for kicks, but for His glory. If the Lord Jesus Christ was only gracious and merciful to the righteous, what glory would he have in proving to the world how compassionate and mighty He really is? When Christ walked the earth, it was not the saints, but the sinners who He ministered to and healed.

I think that God laughs when we make plans. I'm sure He finds it amusing that we actually think that we are in full control of our destinies. Do not get me wrong. We do have *some* power to make choices through our free will, but ultimately, He is in control. At the age of thirty-five, I would have never guessed that I would be having another child. My children are fourteen and sixteen and I was looking forward to giving them the boot in a few more years and regaining my freedom and independence. Yet, here I am starting motherhood all over again, and beginning a new chapter in my life. Have you ever heard the saying, 'never say never'? Well, I encourage all of you to never put the cart before the horse because you never know what the future holds for you. In the past many people predicted the worst of fates concerning me. According to these soothsayers and know it all's, I should have died in 2012, but God had other plans for me. And I believe that He has other plans concerning you. Plans for you to prosper and live, in the name of Jesus. Amen

Come as You Are

I write this letter in the hope that my fellow sinners will come as they are to the throne of our Lord and savior Jesus Christ before it is too late. Many of you think that your sins are too great and piled too high to receive mercy and grace from our Heavenly Father, but that is far from the truth. The God of Creation searches for His lost sons and daughters and eagerly awaits their return. The fifteenth chapter of Luke tells us the story of a man with two sons. The younger son asks his father for his share of the inheritance and his father gives it to him gladly. The younger son takes his inheritance and goes to a distant country and squanders every last penny of his inheritance by partying and living wild. Later, he hires himself out as a pig farmer because he was so poor. The man was so hungry that he longed to fill his stomach with the slop that the pigs ate because nobody gave him anything to eat. Soon the man finally came to his senses, realizing that his father's servants ate well and had a place to sleep, while he was starving to death. The younger son decides to return to his father, saying, "Father I have sinned against heaven and against you. I am no longer worthy to be called your son." Instead of shunning his son and rejecting him, the father was filled with compassion for him and kissed him. Then the father ordered his servants to bring his younger son the best rob and put a ring on his finger and sandals on his feet. In addition, the father held a feast in the younger son's honor, saying, "For this son of mine was dead and is alive again; he was lost and is found."

Why do you think that Jesus tells us this story of the Prodigal Son? I believe it was to illustrate God's mercy and grace towards lost sinners. His holy Word tells us that "There is rejoicing in the presence of God over one sinner who repents (Luke 15:10). No matter how far we stray and no matter what we have done or are still doing, our Heavenly father wants us to return to Him and will except us just as we are because He loves us that much. Unlike the love of men, God's love is pure and unconditional with no strings attached. Whoever comes to Him, He will never cast out (John 6:37). Look at me, one who has broken every commandment, but one. Regardless of all of my past sins, God accepted me as I was- wretched and out of order. I can tell you this without shame because the Lord has redeemed me. I am not at all concerned about how you view or perceive me, but I am only concerned about what the God of Creation thinks of me. If God be the forgiver of sins, then why worry over useless opinions of men and women who cannot? Since we all know that there is nothing new under the sun that God has not seen before, do not be cocky enough to think that your sins are different or greater than the next man's because at the end of the day, sin is sin- point blank, period. Our spirit man has been beaten down and crushed by Satan's lies for far too long. Let's stand up and dust our spirits off, then come as we are to the cross of Jesus Christ. How much longer shall He wait for your return?

How to Develop a Relationship with Christ

Developing a relationship with Jesus Christ is simpler than we may think and only requires that we call on His name. The best was to get to know Him is by speaking to Him, either alone or with a group of likeminded people. If you have never spoken to Jesus before, it may seem weird the first few times you try it, but I can assure you that it will become easier and like second nature, after a while. I would like you to think of getting to know Christ in the same way that we would get to know a new neighbor, co-worker or friend. The benefit is that Christ Jesus will turn out to be the truest and loyal friend of anyone you have ever met on earth or will ever meet. And if having a relationship with Christ will certainly benefit you in this life, just wait until the second life begins!

Though there are several ways to communicate with the God of Creation, always remember that you must go through His Son Jesus Christ to get to Him. Be sure to add 'in the name of Jesus' at the beginning or end of every conversation or prayer. You may talk to or pray to God anywhere you are (at church, in the car, in the shower, on the toilet, while mowing grass, at work, at a friend's, while shopping or out jogging, etc.,) and in any way that you like (in your head, aloud, on your knees, lying or sitting down, hands raised, etc.).

I have discussed with you how to develop a relationship with Christ through dialog, but I have also composed a list highlighting the importance of developing such a relationship with our Lord and savior which includes both pros and cons:

PROS:

- Salvation: The gift of eternal life
- True Guidance
- Power
- Prosperity
- Having a true friend who will never turn His back on you no matter what you do
- Unconditional love
- Sense of fulfillment
- Avoidance of hell (no second death)

CONS:

- The destroyer (Satan) will harass you
- People may dislike you
- You may experience hardships in the first life

Where Are the Righteous?

Lord **Almighty,** in the bible you speak of 7,000 people who have not bended their knee to Baal (Kings 19:18). Where are they? Now, I know how the prophet Elijah felt when he sat lonely in his cave. These feelings of loneliness are foreign to me, as I have always been somewhat of a loner, but I now feel indeed alone for the first time in my life and it saddens me. Father God, so many have come against me without cause, but for the sake of your name. Many have plotted on me, devising underhanded schemes to lead me astray and pull or slow me down. Strangers have even taken up the cause to persecute and abuse my body at every turn for their advantages. Everywhere I go, the wicked ready themselves to exploit me. They victimize me, then tell me in indirect ways that I should not play the victim. Their actions are not only detestable, but laughable at best.

How can I escape the snares of the wicked when I am forced to dwell among them to put food on my table and provide for my children? Lord, how can I escape the negative energy that some people intentionally dump in my lap when I go out in public? I pray that you will see my affliction and persecution that I suffer in your Holy Name and have mercy on me Heavenly Father. I hold onto the hope that after a while, you will make a way for me to survive in this wicked world without much more undue pain and suffering.

Lord, have I ever lifted my hand to cause my neighbor pain? If I have, then I deserve this lot. Have I ever intentionally afflicted them? If so, then their wrath against me is just. Have I ever lifted my voice to slander my fellow kinsmen? If so, then their lies against me would be karmic. No, my hands are clean against them, but not against you, Lord. You redeemed my life from the grave and gave me a second chance, yet I still sinned like an ignorant, disobedient child. Could this be the reason that I am still in the valley crawling on all four like a beast? I have since repented and changed my ways. I hardly leave the house for fear that I may be tempted, led astray or taken advantage of by the numerous wolves in sheep's clothing. I have separated myself from those proudly living in sin until I can figure out how to witness to them without backsliding.

Father God, where are the 7,000 who like me, have an earnest zeal for you and our Lord and Savior Jesus Christ? Has the enemy intentionally scattered us? I pray that you will see that my repentance is genuine and lessen your chastening, for I have learned my lesson. I am no longer a slave to sin, but to the One True Living God. I live and will die for you, Lord Almighty without hesitation. In you, I put my hope and my trust. If I never meet a soul who is fully committed to you and am forced to live a life of solitude, I will do so with gladness of heart. I am not complaining to you, Lord, but am speaking out of sorrow. You tell us to cast all of our cares burdens and fears onto you because you care, Lord Jesus. I ask these questions not to be smart or worrisome, but to gain clarity and understanding regarding my condition. I am confident that your Word is the truth and that after some time, you will stretch out your hand to elevate me from my lowly position.

you will make me whole and established at last. It has been three years that I have undergone much persecution, hardships, trial, tribulations and tests (some of which I did not pass), but still I hold onto my faith in the Father God of Creation, the Son and the Holy Spirit. If I have to endure another three hundred years of the same for the sake of my Lord and savior Jesus Christ, I will do it. Even so, where are the 7,000 of whom you spoke of? Are they now gone, and I am alone? No. I will never truly be alone so long as I have You. I will follow You till the end of my days and beyond, in Jesus name. Amen

Don't Blame God

I **write this letter because** I know that many of you blame the God of Creation for all of your earthy woes. You have lost your sons, daughters, mothers, fathers, sisters and brothers in deaths that might have been horrific, and you ask yourselves why has God allowed these things to happen. You want to know where God was when tragedy struck you? To answer you, I tell you that He was on high in the same place that He was when His Only Son died in the hands of the wicked, also. There are some things that I wish to tell you with all the gentleness that I can muster from my heart because I know that you have been through a lot. I know of your pain and suffering intimately, because I too have suffered many of the same losses, but know this: God still loves you and He cares about you. In anger and bitterness, you may have cursed His Holy Name. You may have stopped believing in Him and have even set your hearts against Him in hate, but His love for you is still undying and unconditional. Unlike people, who are quick to go off the deep end and loose hope when things go wrong, our Lord and savior is patient, forgiving and His love endures forever.

In the world we live in, both good and evil exists. God is

good and Satan is evil. It is only when we understand the
origins of evil that we fully recognize who is truly responsible
for our problems. Have you ever heard anyone blame the devil
for his hand in tragic events? Most likely you have not. Satan
is all too happy that your displaced anger, bitterness and
resentment is directed not at him, but at God. I can only
imagine Satan sitting in the corner of our room laughing at us.
The devil knows that our anger only separates us from the love
of God Almighty and destroys our faith, which is the key to
salvation. This is just the kind of thing that the devil counts
on. Ungodly anger only gives the devil a foothold in our lives
(Ephesians 4:27).

It is ironic too me that when good things happen in our
lives, we are quick to attribute it to our own doing or
achievements, but as soon as something bad happens, we are
quick to blame God. Suddenly, we lose confidence in His
ability to control the people and events in our lives, but in
reality, He is fully in control. Satan took everything from Job
from material possessions to his family, but Job still refused to
curse God, praising Him instead (Book of Job). Rather than
becoming angry, bitter and resentful towards God, we should
humble ourselves enough to cry out to the Lord, casting all of
our cares, fears, grief and pain onto Him, as Job did, who
suffered the greatest of losses. The bible warns us that in this
world, there will be trouble (John 16:33), yet we still think that
we deserve to be immune from unpleasant circumstances.

Please understand that God may not be the cause of your
misfortune, but He may allow certain things to happen in our
lives. Often times, He allows us to experience obstacles, trials
and tribulations to test our faith in Him or strengthen us. Keep
in mind that whatever Satan has stolen from you, that the God
of Creation can restore to you tenfold. Everything our just
Heavenly Father does is for a reason and for our good, even
when we cannot see it or comprehend His perfect will. Satan

has taken enough from us. Do not allow him to also take away your hope in Him who created you also.

We Are All Slaves (Who's Your Daddy?)

How would you feel if I told you that we are all slaves (or servants, if you will)? Well, sorry to break your hearts, but that is exactly what we are. Before you take up arms, alleging that you are free, remember that even the Son of Man did not come to be served, but to serve and give His life as a ransom for many (Mark 10:45).

Be it slaves to work, sex, gambling, addiction; or slaves of Satan, Jesus Christ; or whatever or whoever else, we are all slaves to something or someone. That said, I encourage all of you to choose a kindly master, not one who will lie to you and deceive you to the grave. Start thinking about where you would like to spend eternity after the first death. Life here on earth is so short. Our focus should be on how we can make the most of it. Either we will choose to be slaves to what is good or

"The human being is a self-propelled automaton entirely under the control of external influences. Willful and predetermined as they appear, his actions are governed not from within, but without. He is like a float tossed about by the waves of a turbulent sea."
-Nikola Tesla

what is bad; what is godly or what is ungodly. Friends, please be sure that whatever or whoever you are a slave to, does not steer you wrong. That is all.

Be Happy

Our Heavenly Father wants nothing more for His children, but for us to love one another and be happy. We only have a short time to spend on earth, so do not spend it in distress and misery, but make the most of your lives by living it in happiness. Anger, resentment and depression only bring on wrinkles and an early death, while love, peace and happiness brings us life.

A study on Italian Americans in Roseto, Pennsylvania was conducted by scientist who could not figure out why the Italian residents lived longer than other Americans. Heart disease, the number one cause of death in the United States, was not affecting Roseto, which was predominately Italian American at the time of the study in1961. Scientist discovered that the residents of Roseto ate whatever they pleased and had a diet that was

"Happiness depends upon ourselves."
-Aristotle

"God can't give us peace and happiness apart from Him because there is no such thing."
-C. S. Lewis

high in cholesterol and fat. They did not exercise much, nor did they not concern themselves with health matters much at all. After hundreds of extensive interviews, these baffled scientists concluded that good living contributed to the longevity of the lives of the Italian Americans who lived in Roseto. The close family ties that the residents shared allowed them to feel happy and secure.

We have all heard stories about grandparents who are sometimes driven to an early grave behind raising their children's unruly kids. We have also heard stories of those who have died of grief and loneliness shortly after their spouse passed on. Day after day, week after week and year after year, we toil, struggle and strive to earn a living and make ends meet, but what good does that do us if we cannot even enjoy the fruits of our labor? The masses toil every day and many of us cannot even afford to take a vacation or spend quality time with our families. Quit slaving all the day long to earn money which we then hand right back to the masters who gave it to us, via bills. I do not encourage you to neglect your bills, but I *do* encourage everyone to first choose their families and their happiness over the same. A stack of unpaid bills cannot kill a person, but a person can work themselves to death paying them or stressing about them. Friends, I beg you to take the time to find what happiness really means to you and pursue it. Let hope, faith and peace (which are free) be the most valued asset that we strive for. It is the Lord Almighty's will that we purse happiness. Nothing is better for a man than that he should eat, drink and that his soul should enjoy his good labor (Ecclesiastes 2:24).

Get Your Household in Order

Getting your house in order has to do with preparedness for the return of the Lord Jesus Christ. This not only pertains to our physical homes, but also our mind, body and spirit. No man on earth, nor the angels in heaven or even Jesus Christ Himself knows the day or hour of His return, but only the Father (Mark 13:32). Therefore, we must confess and repent of our sins, renewing our mind, body and souls to prepare for our savior. If the master of the house knew what hour the thief would come, he would have watched and not allowed his house to be broken into (Matthew 24:43). Christ has told us that He too, would come back as a thief in the night, so we must pray and keep watch.

Getting our house in order starts with and within us. Turn from your wicked ways, and start doing what is right. If you are a parent or someone in

"I have been impressed with the urgency of doing. Knowing is not enough; we must apply. Being willing is not enough; we must do."
-Leonardo da Vinci

"The future belongs to those who prepare for it today."
-Malcolm X

a leadership role, how can you expect to manage your children or those under you if you cannot even manage yourself? We cannot expect our children or others we have authority to guide to listen us, if we do not even listen our God who created us, and sees all of us as His children. Now, we all know of meddlesome people who enjoy concerning themselves with the households of others. Meanwhile their spouse is having an affair, their children are unruly, their brother or sister is struggling with an addiction and their own house is in shambles. Instead of taking care of their own affairs, they are too busy concerning themselves with your business. Do not be that nosy, meddlesome neighbor, but rather first clean your own house. Until we do so, we will never be in a position to go back and assist our neighbors who indeed need our help. This does not mean to selfishly neglect our brothers and sisters. We pray for them and give them warnings before continuing to manage our own affairs until we can further aid them.

Our houses require constant maintenance that we must stay on top of, lest there be a breach in the order. At times when my house was running smoothly, I let people come into it who disrupted that order, and chaos and turmoil ensued. I would become sick and depressed and my children would start acting out, even taking on the foul characteristics of those whom I allowed into my home. I worshipped less and my motivation to work for God lessened. Had I been watchful, I would have never allowed the wicked to infiltrate my team (family). I was so busy enjoying the peace that God had gifted me that I, the door keeper, had fallen asleep. Learn from my mistake friends, and stay awake! When we cleanse our house of unclean spirits and they go out seeking rest and find none, they will undoubtedly try to return to you. And that spirit comes and finds your house swept and put in order, he goes and takes seven other more spirits more wicked than himself and enters our home (Luke 11:24-26). I urge you to make no provisions for these unclean spirits or people to come into your household.

In closing, I cannot stress to you enough how crucial getting your house in order is. Though we do not know when Christ will return, blessed is the servant who his master will find doing as he should when he comes. Be diligent and present yourselves approved to God, as a worker who does not need to be ashamed (2 Timothy 2:15). It is the faithful and dutiful servant who reaps the rewards. We all know what the God of creation expects of us and therefore, we have no excuse not to be prepared. When the King comes knocking, we should be ready.

Striving for Righteousness and Sainthood

Achieving **righteousness and sainthood** is forever a work in progress. If being without sin is a prerequisite, then the goal would be unreachable, for no one is without sin, not one. While righteousness can be accounted to us by faith (as it was to Abraham), sainthood can only be contributed to one who lives a morally virtuous life that is pleasing to God. Thus, I believe that sainthood should not be appointed to anyone by man, but by the God of Creation Himself, who chooses the saint.

In my pursuit of righteousness and sainthood, I have found there to be a transformation of heart and former way of living. In walking with Christ Jesus, He has changed my mind so that I no longer do many of the things I formerly did or live as I used to. In

"A return to first principles in a republic is sometimes caused by the simple virtue of one man. His good examples have such an influence that the good men strive to imitate him, and the wicked are ashamed to lead a life so contrary to his example."
-Niccolo Machiavelli

achieving righteousness and sainthood, one must also be willing to face the slings and arrows of persecution for their faith in Him, in this world. I believe that to live a sinless life is difficult, but not impossible. In any case, to achieve such a lifestyle is (and will be) forever a work in progress.

"Consider your origins: you were not made to live as brutes, but to follow virtue and knowledge."
-Dante Alighieri

"Piety requires us to honor truth above our friends."
-Aristotle

How Far Are You Willing to Go? (Till Death Do Us Part)

Just how much do you love the Lord Jesus Christ? I know that we profess with our mouths that we love Him, but exactly how far are you willing to go for Christ to receive the gift of eternal life? Many of you have taken the oath of 'till death do us part' with your spouses, but would you be willing to get your head chopped off to save their life? Well, you very well may get beheaded for your belief in Jesus Christ. Are you willing to suffer persecution, trials, tribulation and even possibly die for the sake of the Name? I do not want to frighten you, but as true believers in Jesus Christ, these are some legitimate questions that you should ask yourselves.

I know some people who refuse to read the book of Revelations in the

"The fact is that a man who wants to act virtuous in every way necessarily comes to grief among so many who are not virtuous."
-Niccolo Machiavelli

bible because they fear the ending days on earth, but those who truly believe in Christ have absolutely nothing at all to fear. Besides, Christ Himself tells us "And do not fear those who kill the body, but cannot kill the soul. But rather fear Him who is able to destroy both soul and body in hell (Matthew 10:28)." Even still, I admit that I have prayed to the Lord to lift me up prior to the time that the tribulations are to take place. I have done this not out of fear, but because I do not wish to see the suffering of my brothers and sisters, nor the masses who will find it easier to take the mark of the beast, than to fight for their lives- the lives that Jesus died on the cross for. For the scripture says, "Whoever believes on Him will not be put to shame (Romans 10:11) and whoever calls on the name of the Lord will be saved (Romans10:13). That means when the sword is hanging above your head or the gun is pointed at your skull, that we should not deny Christ, as it is written: "Therefore, whoever confesses Me before men, him I will also confess before My Father who is in heaven. But whoever denies me before men, I will also deny before My Father who is in heaven (Matthew 10:32-33)." Jesus also goes on to say that "He who loses his life for my sake will find it

"There is no easy walk to freedom anywhere, and many of us will have to pass through the valley of the shadow of death again and again before we reach the mountaintop of our desires."
-Nelson Mandela

"Firstly, do not fear hardship, and secondly, do not fear death."
-Mao Tse-tung

(Matthew 10:39)." It will only take a spit second to make a life damning or lifesaving decision, but that choice is yours, and yours alone.

The Atheist Challenge

Hey you **Atheist** or other nonbelievers in Christ Jesus, how are you? I hope this letter finds you in good spirits because I care about you, despite our difference in beliefs. I knew my book would end up in your hands (in fact, I prayed it would), just as the bible that you do not believe in has. I have created this challenge for non-believers in the God of Creation and the Lord Jesus Christ, as well as others who walk the fine line between belief and unbelief, as I once did. Some of the things I will ask you to do may be difficult for you, hence that is why I used the word challenge. I am challenging you to open your hearts and minds to something new and exciting; something positive and productive that will change your lives for the better, if not save it. Many of

"There are three classes of people: Those who see, those who see when they are shown, those who do not see."
-Leonardo da Vinci

"Just as no one can be forced into belief, so no one can be forced into unbelief."
-Sigmund Freud

you spend so much time disputing the existence of what you do not believe in, and I now challenge you to put some of that same energy into seeking the truth.

The Challenge:

First, get on your knees and confess your sins and repent for them, asking the God of Creation to forgive you for them. Next, seek God through prayer once daily, either before you go to sleep or early in the morning before you start your hectic day. In prayer, ask God to reveal Himself to you in a way that cannot be denied. Tell God that you are inviting Him into your heart and into your home. Admit to God that you do not believe in His existence, but that you are open minded enough to look for the truth (God already knows this about you, but He delights in the confessions of your mouth). Tell Him that you truly want to get to know Him, if He does in fact exist. Then, dump all of your anxieties, cares, fears, hopes and dreams into God's lap. Be sure to begin or end each prayer with 'in the name of Jesus Christ,' so that your prayers will reach Him, for no man comes to the Father, except through Jesus Christ, the Son (John14:6).

In addition to opening the doors of communication with the God who created you through prayer, I challenge you to try to do the right thing throughout your day. That does not mean you have to be perfect- that we can never be. Instead simply respecting your neighbor and yourself will suffice. Lastly, I challenge you to (dare I say it) read your bible, if you have one. If not perhaps you can borrow one. You do not have to read the whole thing in one sitting, but maybe you can start by just reading a few verses once or twice each week. Since the King James Version is difficult for most people to understand because of the lingo, try the New International

Version, which is more comprehendible to beginners. The book of Romans and Matthew are not only my favorite books in the bible, but I believe they provide the most insight about Jesus Christ, so start there. Do all of these things for forty days and God will do the rest. Do not be surprised to see that God will not only show up, but He will show out, changing your life forever.

I hope that you enjoyed reading 40 Days & 40 Nights A Saint. Of all the books I have written, and will write in the future, I expect that this one might be the most controversial. I understand that some of my experiences and beliefs may not resonate with some of you and therefore, might be impossible to grasp. Yet I must stand in truth anyway. I have tried to be as gentle as possible in expressing my views as it pertains to the Word of God and salvation through Jesus Christ without alienating you. That said, I did not sugar-coat anything for you either. Regardless of whether or not we see eye to eye on the topics I have written about, rather than slander and slay me, your prayers concerning me will do just nicely. At the end of the day, if this book has brought one soul (if not more) closer to the truth in Jesus Christ, then my goal has been achieved. I pray for you all so that together we might be healed. Amen

"There are times when you have to be strong, and times when you have to stand alone for what you believe in."
-Queen Latifah

WORKS CITED

Alighieri, Dante, *Inferno*. Wadsworth Editions, 1998.

Alighieri, Dante, *The Paradiso of Dante*. Longman, Orme, Brown, Green and Longman, 1840.

Alighieri, Dante, *The Devine Comedy: Inferno*. Simon and Shuster, May 1, 2005.

Aristotle, The Nicomachean Ethics of Aristotle: with English Notes. Henry Slatter, 1836.

ASPI MISTRY, *The Whale of Time*. Partridge Publishing, 2013.

Bender, Narim, *Leonardo da Vinci: What He Said*. BookRix, September 15, 2013.

Campbell, Stan and Bell, James, *The Complete Idiot's Guide to the Book of Revelations*. Penguin, December 1, 2001.

Cheney, Margaret et. al., *Tesla: Man Out of Time*. Barnes and Noble Publishing, 1999.

Coelho, Paulo, *Aleph*. Alfred A. Knopf, 2011.

Coren, Michael, *C.S. Lewis: The Man Who Created Narnia*. Ignatius Press, February 1, 2006.

Da Vinci, Leonardo, *Leonardo's Notebooks*. Black Dog Leventhal Publishers, August 1, 2005.

Du Bois, W.E.B., *John Brown: A Biography*. Random House Publishing, July 21, 2010.

Farley, John, *On the Beach with Dave Chappelle*. Time Magazine, May 15, 2005

Freud, Sigmund, *Civilization and Its Discontents*. W. W. Norton & Company, September 17. 1989. Freud

Greene, Robert, 48 Laws of *Power*. Penguin Books, September 1, 2000

Hagopian Institute, Quote Junkie Presidents Edition. Hagopian Institute, March 12, 2008.

Hughes, Langston and Hubbard, Dolan, *The Collected Works of Langston Hughes: Essays on Art, Race, Politics and World Affairs*. University of Missouri Press, 2002.

Keller, Kristin Thoennes, *Malcolm X: Force for Change*. Capstone, July 1, 2005.

King, Martin Luther, *A Testament of Hope: The Essential Writings and speeches of Martin Luther*. HarperCollins, December 7, 1990.

Latifah, Queen, *Put On Your Crown: Life Changing Moments on the Path to Queendom*. Grand Central Publishing, May 6, 2010.

Lavid, Linda A., *Publishing Tips: Weekly Strategies for the Independent Writer*. Authorship, 2008.

Machiavelli, Niccolo, *The Prince*. Open Road Media, July 1, 2014.

Machiavelli, Niccolo, *The Historical, Political and Diplomatic Writings of Niccolo Machiavelli*. C.E. Detmold, 1882.

Mandela, Nelson, *Long Walk to Freedom: The Autobiography of Nelson Mandela*. Little, Brown, March 11, 2008.

Mandela, Nelson, *Speech at Rice University*. 1999.
Manning, Brennan, *The Ragamuffin Gospel*, Crown Publishing Group, August 19. 2008.

Nguyen, Trung, *Naturalopy Precept 17: Forgiveness*. Ecognitive.com, January 15, 2015.

Palahniuk, Chuck, *Lullaby*. Knopf Doubleday Publishing Group, July 29, 2003.

Pool, Hannah, *Interview with Paulo Coelho*. The Gaurdian, March 18, 2009.

148

Prawdin, Michael, *The Mongol Empire: Its Rise & Legacy*. Transaction Publishers, 1940.

Rockefeller, John, *John D. Rockefeller on Making Money: Advice and Words of Wisdom on Building and Sharing Wealth*. Skyhorse Publishing, Inc., May 31, 2005.

Rosenfels, Paul, *Freud and the Scientific Method*. Ninth Street Center, 1980.

RuPaul, *Workin' It!: RuPaul's Guide to Life Liberty and the Pursuit of Style*. Harper Collins, February 2, 2010.

Samuels, Allison, *Facing the Music*. Newsweek, September 25, 2005.

Saint Augustine, *City of God, Volume 1*. T & T Clark. 1888.

Selassie, Haile, *Selassie's Speech on Inaction in Addis Ababa*. 1963Selassie, Haile, *Selassie's Address to the United Nations*. October 6, 1963.

Shakespeare, William, *Julius Caesar*. Courier Corporation, 1991.

Students' Academy, *Words of Wisdom: Lao Tzu*. Lulu Press, January 27, 2015.

Students' Academy, *Words of Wisdom: Sigmund Freud*. Lulu Press, Inc., September 1, 2014.

Tesla, Nikola, *Radio Power Will Revolutionize the World*. Modern Mechanics and Inventions Magazine, July 1934.

Tesla, Nikola, *The Problem of Increasing Human Energy*. Century Illustrated Magazine, June 1900.

Tesla, Nikola, *A Means for Furthering Peace*. Electrical World and Engineer, January 7, 1905.

The Holy Bible (New International Version).

Tse-tung, Mao, *Quotations from Chairman Moa Tse-tung*. Barnes & Noble Publishing, February 12, 2008.

Tzu, Sun, *The Art of War*. Axiom, 2002.

Warren, Rick, *The Purpose Driven Life: What Am I Here For?* Zondervan Publishing, October 23, 2012.

Wesley, John, *The Works of Reverend John Wesley, A.M.* J. Emory, B B Waugh, for the Methodist Episcopal Church, J. Collard, printer 1831.

Winfrey, Oprah, *Forgive So You Can Truly Live*. Huffpost, November 11, 2012.

Young, William Paul, *The Shack*. Windblown Media, June 1, 2011.

INDEX

SPECIAL PREVIEW

HEAR MY TESTIMONY

"Whoa!"

I clung to a complete stranger to prevent myself from falling flat on my face after tripping over air. With the exception of spiked eggnog on Christmas, I rarely drank- but tonight I had to drink the whole bottle of Cisco just to build up enough courage to do what I was about to do.

I couldn't believe that I was about to do this, but desperate times, calls for desperate measures. I thought about my 4 year old son and 2 year old daughter who slept at home unattended. As guilty as I felt about leaving them at home alone, I refused to let them wake up in the morning with no food to eat. The guilt I felt about leaving my children almost made me turn around and go home. After all, I was more than confident that they wouldn't wake up until long after I had returned, but suppose there was a fire? I allowed my mind to think the worst.

I stood on the crossroads of indecisiveness being tugged between my inner intuition which was losing the battle against the intoxicating effects of the alcohol. I shivered as the brutal east coast winds blew my hair in every direction, threatening to carry me off. If I didn't get my hands on some money quick, my children and I would get to know this harsh climate intimately, as we would soon be homeless on top of hungry.

My situation was do or die. Surrounded by the people, bright lights and flashing neon signs on the street, I felt like I was in New York City, rather than the dirty, dark and grimy streets of Baltimore. I couldn't help but laugh out loud. My whole life had been a rollercoaster ride full of sharp turns and twists. I wondered when the conductor would finally let me get off the ride. Fueled by desperation, I looked up at the three story building that was in front of me.

"I'm already here so I may as well make the most of it," I said aloud, to psych myself out and get pumped.

The devil was beckoning me to come inside for a slice of devil's pie. I was now entering his domain- his house. Stepping inside, I prayed that when I came out, I would be left unchanged, unstained. I was about to undergo a baptism by fire.

SPECIAL PREVIEW SECTION FEATURE

Best Selling Author of *The Tears I've Cried: A Personal Memoir*, Makaila Renee delivers the long awaited sequel *Hear My Testimony*, the continuing story of a girl's search for the love of a family.

Physically, emotionally, and psychologically abused by her parents, Renee struggles to make enough money to pay for her own apartment and save up for a college education. A young girl who has never had a loving home, Renee is swept off her feet when she meets Semaj, a slick-talking womanizer from the South. Things finally start looking up for Renee until her cousin Roxanne comes to live with her. After catching Semaj and Roxanne in bed together, Renee's world is torn apart all over again! An unwed mother in dire straits, Renee turns to the strip club to make big money and find a way out of the slums.

In search of stability, little does she know, that the real hurt is just beginning…

Hear My Testimony is a raw, page turning true story of sex, lies, money and murder in the name of survival. The sequel, *Hear My Testimony* is an inspirational, yet gripping account of a child fighting to cope with her past and refusing to let it hold her hostage.

Reserve your personally autographed copy of *Hear My Testimony*, the sequel to *The Tears I've Cried: A Personal Memoir*, available May, 2016.

Visit   WWW.MAKAILARENEE.COM   for preordered copies or to DONATE to The Broke Writer's Fund, supporting local writer's.